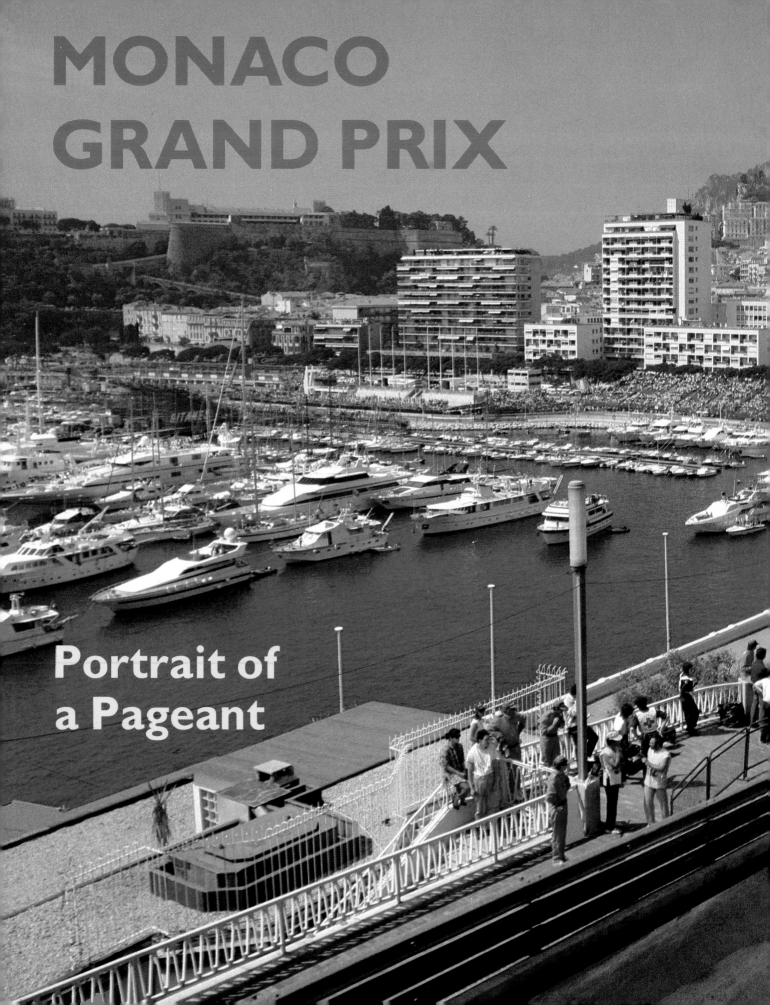

MONACO GRAND PRIX

Portrait of a Pageant

Featuring the
photography of
MICHAEL HEWETT
Text by
CRAIG BROWN
and **LEN NEWMAN**

To JEAN, PIERS and ALISON

First published in 1989 by
MOTOR RACING PUBLICATIONS LTD
Unit 6, The Pilton Estate
46 Pitlake, Croydon CR0 3RY
England

Copyright © 1989 Motor Racing Publications Ltd

ISBN 0 947981 30 6

Photoset in Great Britain by
Tek-Art Typesetting Ltd, West Wickham, Kent
Printed and bound in Hong Kong by
Bookbuilders Ltd

Contents

Introduction	7	1964: BRM 1-2 – Again	64
A Photographer in Monaco	8	1965: Classic Hill	66
Pageantry and Charisma	12	1966: Formula for Success?	68
One Man's Dream	19	1967: A Race in Shadow	70
Refining the Layout	23	1968: Cosworth's First Monaco	76
1929: 'Williams' Opens the Record Book	28	1969: Hill Makes Five	80
1930: Bugatti Clean Sweep	30	1970: Last Minute Rindt	86
1931: Sweet Revenge for Chiron	32	1971: Stewart All the Way	90
1932: The Italian Challenge	33	1972: No Overtaking	94
1933: Incident and Accident	34	1973: Monaco Facelift	98
1934: A New Formula	36	1974: Peterson in Charge	102
1935: Three-Pointed Star Ascending	38	1975: Forza Ferrari!	104
1936: German Offensive	39	1976: More Track, More Cylinders, More Wheels	108
1937: Mercedes Invincible	40	1977: Wolf in Full Cry	112
1948: First Postwar Win to Farina	41	1978: Dependable Depailler	118
1950: Easy Win for Fangio	42	1979: Ferrari Foremost	122
1952: Sports Car Diversion	43	1980: First Win for Williams	128
1955: Grand Prix d'Europe	44	1981: Turbo Triumph	132
1956: Fine Victory for Moss	46	1982: The Winner? Who, Me?	136
1957: Fangio on Form	48	1983: Slick Decision	142
1958: A Turning Tide	48	1984: Red Light to Red Flag	148
1959: First Win for Brabham	50	1985: Prost Again	154
1960: A Race of Attrition	51	1986: McLaren Streets Ahead	160
1961: Moss: A Touch of Genius	53	1987: Senna Takes an Active Interest	166
1962: V8 v V6	54	1988: The Prost and Senna Show	174
1963: BRM Benefit	56	Winners and Losers	184

Monaco in the 1960s with high-rise buildings beginning to alter the backcloth to the Grand Prix. No-one tried harder to win the race than Jim Clark in his Lotus, right, but success would always elude them, here in 1964 because of fading oil pressure.

Introduction

This book was born out of more than a quarter of a century of dedicated effort by a gifted photographer. Michael Hewett's work has been widely published in motor racing annuals and magazines, but this is the first time he has had the opportunity to make a personal choice from his extensive archive. The pictures which form the heart of this book are his own selection, chosen in many cases on their technical merit, but sometimes for the memories they provoke, either of the race itself or of the photographic challenge.

His sparing use of the telephoto lens is a hallmark of Hewett's technique, which has enabled him through this portfolio of pictures to capture the atmosphere not just of a famous motor race but of the total pageantry of the Monaco Grand Prix. His artistry with the camera, perhaps demonstrated most vividly in the demanding discipline of black-and-white photography, does much to explain why thousands of motor racing enthusiasts, having witnessed this remarkable event at first hand, find its magnetism irresistible and return year after year to the Principality.

Michael Hewett's photography of the Monaco Grand Prix began in 1962, but the race itself dates back to 1929, which is why other photographic sources have been used to illustrate the earlier years of the Grand Prix so as to complete the pictorial coverage of this most famous of all Formula 1 races. Short reviews of each Grand Prix have been added to support and supplement the photography and a full list of race results and statistics is provided at the end of the book to identify the victors and the not so successful, year by year, as well as the margin of the victory on each occasion.

As the Monaco Grand Prix reaches its half-century, the excitement, drama and colour which unfold on the following pages stand as a tribute to Antony Noghes, whose dream it was to create a 'round the houses' motor race through the streets of Monte Carlo; of the Automobile Club de Monaco, who saw his dream become reality; and of the House of Grimaldi, whose patronage of this unique sporting occasion is continued today with such enthusiasm by His Serene Highness Prince Rainier III.

Acknowledgements

My warmest thanks go to Rosie and Jean-Louis Bernard, of the Chatham Bar, Monte Carlo, for their invaluable help, also to Jean-Marie Moll, of the Palace Archives, Monaco, not only for his professional expertise, but especially for his personal interest.

I am also indebted to Messrs Rosset, Aubry and Laforgère, of the Département Co-ordination et Preservation du Patrimoine Historique, la Société des Bains de Mer, Monte Carlo; to my friend Pete Wainwright, in recognition of his work in classifying the material; and finally to my brother, Brian Hewett, for his foot-slogging round Paris and Monaco on my behalf.

MICHAEL HEWETT

A Photographer in Monaco

The most remarkable point about Michael Hewett's photographs, aside from their sheer dramatic impact, is that they are not the work of a seasoned professional armed with the latest equipment, but an example of the craft of a dedicated, gifted amateur, for whom composition and technique are the essence of success. Even if his strenuous business commitments did not preclude his attendance at other Grands Prix, Michael doubts if he would follow the Formula 1 'circus' from country to country. Ever since June 3, 1962, when he stood on Monte Carlo station in the evening sunshine after photographing his first Grand Prix and wondered if he would one day return to this magical race, the lure of Monaco has held for him a unique attraction. In the 27 intervening years he has never missed a Monaco Grand Prix.

In 1962, of course, Michael Hewett was completely unknown to the race organizers, and the only way he could hope to find a worthwhile vantage point was to get up as early as possible on the Sunday morning and be at the trackside before the other spectators could beat him to the best places. Whether by luck, intuition or premonition, he headed for the Gasworks hairpin, which in those days was the first corner after the start line. Within seconds of the start, the famous first-lap shunt, in which three cars were instantly eliminated, occurred right in front of him; Michael's photographs of the accident were his first to be published.

In Grand Prix racing, nothing stands still for long, and that includes the photographer. Michael quickly realized that in order to make the most of the opportunities available he would have to be able to move freely around the circuit. He therefore sent a selection of his Gasworks hairpin photographs to the Automobile Club de Monaco, asking if he might be issued with a press photographer's pass. Recognizing the value of publicity for their prestigious race, the Club duly obliged, and in 1963 a delighted Michael Hewett was admitted to the elite ranks of the official motor racing photographer, a status he has deservedly enjoyed ever since.

He well remembers the excitement of his first 'official' Monaco Grand Prix. 'Waiting for the start, camera raised, adrenalin pumping, I didn't realize that I was breathing on the back of the camera. When the cars appeared, I moved for my first shot and found I couldn't see a thing because my hot breath had completely fogged the viewfinder. Now I always remember, when I'm not taking or framing a picture, to hold the camera well away from my mouth.'

Inevitably, with the intensification of safety standards in Formula 1 and the enormous increase in the numbers of official photographers seeking prime positions around a confined circuit, the attitude of the Monaco marshals to photographers has changed considerably over the years. This is understandable, but it makes the photographer's job more difficult.

'Up to the late sixties,' Hewett points out, 'you were able to nip across the track at certain points during the race, having first signalled your intention to the marshals.' There were only a very few places where this could safely be accomplished, and one of his favourites was the old station hairpin, one of the slowest parts of the course. 'You could watch the cars and note any gap between them, making sure that the gap was constant for a few laps, and then just nip across. This was considered quite safe, since the station hairpin was a very slow bend with a relatively slow approach as the cars come out of the Mirabeau and zig-zag downhill towards the station. Then, in the early seventies, this practice was frowned upon, and by the mid-seventies it was totally forbidden. Nowadays, you're not even allowed to cross the track half an hour before the race starts.'

The problems of gaining access to areas considered unsafe by the marshals, but rewarding to the photographer, have never deterred Hewett. In earlier years, he found that he could persuade marshals to relax their rules by approaching them during practice and showing them photographs which he had taken at the previous year's race. When they appreciated what he wanted to do, they were often willing to compromise on race day by allowing him into a prohibited zone on the understanding that he would take a few photographs and then move to a safer place. Also, there were invariably times when, with the race under way and cars hurtling past on the limit, the marshals would forget all about a stray photographer, such was the concentration demanded by their own responsibilities.

However, in 1966 Michael felt it necessary to enlist the support of someone at the Automobile Club de Monaco in order to overcome obstructive officialdom. After he had been refused permission to stand at the exit from the chicane, where he knew he could obtain effective head-on shots, he approached Robert Sobra, then the Chief Press Officer, and was given a letter for presentation to the marshals granting him freedom – within the bounds of reasonable safety – to circulate more freely. Unfortunately, even this dispensation was annulled by later events. After he had taken some splendid photographs of cars negotiating the chicane early in the 1967 race, the Principality was stunned by Lorenzo Bandini's terrible accident on the quayside, and no photographer was ever again allowed to stand at that point.

There are several magnificent photographs in the book showing cars emerging from the tunnel. During the sixties, this was one of Hewett's favourite locations. The cars would hit the sunlight at around 150mph, framed dramatically against the darkness of the tunnel mouth and the rows of light bulbs defining the inner curve. The photographer's technique here was to use a telephoto lens and crouch down in the gutter, aiming through the gap in the Armco barrier as the cars came howling out of the gloom. More recently, the old tunnel has been demolished and replaced by a new construction which lets in more daylight. This may be better for the drivers, but it reduces the photographic impact since the contrasts are subdued. However, it is now possible to photograph cars actually inside the tunnel, which was not practical before.

Although photography is not his main business, Michael is highly self-critical in judging his own work. The 30 rolls of film which he may use during the Monaco weekend sometimes yield only four or five photographs which he considers of sufficient merit for inclusion in his growing library. Nevertheless, some of his results bring him particular satisfaction, and one of his personal favourites of all the pictures in this book shows Elio De Angelis in the JPS Lotus during practice for the 1984 race, climbing the hill to the Casino Square at something approaching 160mph. Michael used a wide-angle lens for this shot in order to capture as much as possible of the unique

9

background, but without telephoto effect he could only present the Lotus in the foreground of the picture by crouching on the path outside the barrier and balancing the camera on top of it. The success of the ploy is self-evident but, with De Angelis on a fast qualifying lap, only a few inches separated his nearside front wheel from Hewett's head.

Michael clearly does not believe that his work can be enhanced by a battery of new and expensive equipment. Since his early years at Monaco he has used two old Pentax Spotmatics for black-and-white photography and a Bronica medium-format camera (which takes 120 film) for colour work. Today, he favours colour over black-and-white, but the faithful Spotmatics still accompany him, their antiquity inviting friendly derision from fellow motor racing photographers.

Strategy and forethought are as essential as the equipment. 'An important aspect of photographing the Monaco event,' he explains, 'is the necessity to plan in advance what you intend to film and where you intend to go, so that you don't end up in a particular place and then find, when there's no time to move anywhere else, that the sun is shining straight into the lens. There are several excellent spots around the circuit from which, owing to the position of the sun, photographs cannot be taken during the actual Grand Prix. These viewpoints have to be visited during morning practice, before the sun moves round, and this explains why a number of the more photogenic locations are seldom pictured on race afternoon. Of course, if it's overcast or wet, these factors no longer apply – remember 1972 and 1984? – but then you've got the problem of trying to change film without letting water into the back of the camera.'

Despite its historical and architectural heritage, Monaco is not immune to change. 'Every time they knock down a building, they replace it with something much bigger and higher and, consequently, you find far greater areas of track thrown into shadow.'

A photographer as meticulous as Michael Hewett cannot afford simply to shoot hundreds of photographs in the course of the weekend in the vague hope that, when he returns home, he will find no mistakes. 'I always take with me a small portable darkroom. Each evening I can develop the day's black-and-white films, and in the morning I can study the dry prints, enabling me to rectify any errors of positioning or technique before I go out again.' Needless to say, he is anxious to preserve his good relationship with the hotel. 'I always make sure that, when the maid brings my breakfast, all the chemical smells have been flushed out of the room!'

While he possesses a large selection of lenses, Hewett tends to be very sparing in his use of telephoto lenses at Monaco. The dramatic De Angelis photograph, mentioned earlier, is a case in point. 'I have never been very keen on using a long telephoto lens at Monaco as you get little or no background – and Monaco is certainly a place for backgrounds. Here, I much prefer a standard or wide-angle lens, moving in close to the subject. This is another reason why Monaco particularly appeals to me, because nowhere else can you get so close to Formula 1 racing cars at speed.'

Inevitably, after more than 25 years as a regular visitor to the Grand Prix, Michael Hewett has formed a number of close and invaluable friendships with officials and residents. Though he naturally has no wish to place individuals in an invidious position by singling them out for mention, he makes no secret of the fact that without the many kindnesses of Rosie and Jean-Louis Bernard, of the famous Chatham Bar, several of the photographs in this book simply could not have been taken.

In May 1989, he will be back at work in the Principality for the first Monaco Grand Prix to be run exclusively for 3.5-litre non-turbo cars. Watching for him on television will be his wife Jean and their two children, Piers and Alison. The family's task, fortunately, will not be quite the 'needle in a haystack' search it sounds, for during the race Michael always wears the same brightly-coloured gold T-shirt to make himself as conspicuous as possible. 'It's the only time I ever wear it,' he says.

Pageantry and Charisma

Monaco at Grand Prix time is a place of conflicts and contrasts. Gleaming white-hulled cruisers bob gently with the swell on the blue waters of the harbour while multi-coloured racing cars hurtle past on the quayside yards away. While sun-bronzed bodies sprawl lazily across the boat decks, the cars' drivers, seemingly oblivious to the Mediterranean sunshine, are thickly-wrapped from head to foot, not an inch of flesh exposed. The tree-lined squares and tastefully ornate buildings in the old town stand and stare in quiet, dignified disbelief as a screaming phalanx of razor-edged projectiles storms through their shadows. Around the narrow, twisting streets where Renault 5s and Citroens recently meandered in the honking traffic, needle-nosed Lotuses, McLarens and Ferraris blast by at upwards of 100 miles an hour, exhausts echoing from the buildings.

For all its excitement and incomparable charisma, the Monaco Grand Prix is surely motor racing's most absurd anachronism. It is illogical, impractical and highly dangerous, and yet it survives and prospers, impervious to swings of social and cultural fashion and changing regulations.

For the paying spectators, Monaco can be no mere motor race. After all, if they go to Silverstone, San Marino or Spa, or almost anywhere else, they may stand in the trackside enclosures or wander freely about the circuit; at Monaco, there are few close vantage points apart from grandstands or hotel balconies. Even in the age of package tours, travel to the Principality is relatively expensive and, once there, subsistence is a costly business. Still, its reputation and its allure are untarnished. Despite the ever-increasing range of motor racing excursions available to the enthusiast, the Monaco Grand Prix remains the most sought-after commodity in the specialist tour organizer's catalogue.

Ask Grand Prix drivers what they think of Monaco, and the replies will be as diverse as they are forthright. When you have to drive it, eyeballs popping, palms bruised by a million bumps and over 2,000 gear changes, this is not a race to allow much scope for indifference. Drivers either hate the place and want to go home as quickly as possible or they love everything about it.

Borne on the advancing tide of commercialism which, in the past 20 years, has steadily transformed the face of Grand Prix racing, a third category of visitors seeks diversion and entertainment in Monte Carlo: the sponsors and their guests. Monaco, surely, might have been purpose-built for the sponsors, for whatever the technical limitations of the circuit and its facilities, as a venue for one of the world's most prestigious international sporting events, it provides a showcase of unequalled magnificence.

Of course, Monaco has long been the most socially self-conscious event in the Grand Prix calendar. The concept of Grand Prix racing as a dynamic commercial spectacle could find no more amenable haven than the glittering little Principality, which has always been a place to see and a place in which to be seen.

Aside from the race itself, it is in the famous hotels and bars of Monte Carlo that the extravaganza finds a natural focus. Here, the changing scene is marked not only by physical alteration – though there has been more than enough of that – but also by a different patronage, bringing with it a newer, brighter, more universal ostentation.

Team owners and managers, quick to recognize Monaco's powerful promotional magnetism, crowd the bars and hotel suites with sponsors and guests and, by careful pre-arrangement, with the drivers upon whose performance and commitment the success of the whole gigantic publicity machine will ultimately depend. In years gone by, such social high spots as the Tip Top Bar or the world-renowned Casino were places where off-duty drivers would mingle enthusiastically, signing autographs and sharing jokes with an adoring but relatively undemanding public. Graham Hill, whose record of five Monaco victories is perhaps unlikely ever to be beaten, was a frequent midnight reveller at the Tip Top.

Grand Prix splendour – Nigel Mansell's turbocharged Williams-Honda passes the palms in Monaco's Casino Square, with the Casino itself and the Hotel de Paris as back-drop in 1986. Left: For many years, the Chatham Bar, halfway up the hill to the Casino, has been a popular meeting place for racing enthusiasts. Rosie, right, and her husband Jean-Louis run it. Bette Hill, left, is an honoured visitor; her husband Graham won the Grand Prix five times.

Today, when Grand Prix racing is a sport by derivation rather than by definition, there is unfortunately little room, and little time, for such harmless informality. Except by appointment, drivers are seldom seen on the social circuit, because their 'free' time is necessarily apportioned to the demands of their teams' sponsors, a professional responsibility as important as driving in the race.

Throughout the year, but at Grand Prix weekend in particular, Monaco is a place where traditional elegance sits tolerantly alongside the brash and the new. Inevitably, in such a prosperous and cosmopolitan corner of the Riviera, the older institutions are themselves not immutable, and the hotels and bars have undergone a series of structural and social changes. The Hotel Beau Rivage, formerly situated beside the hill leading up into the town from Ste Devote, has been replaced by a block of flats, while the old Metropole, where many competing drivers used to stay, has been demolished to make way for a major new business and leisure complex. The old Monte Carlo railway station, from whose approach viaduct countless visitors would catch a first tantalizing glimpse of the circuit, was closed down over 20 years ago and its site is now occupied by the Loews Hotel. Beyond the circuit confines, the newer Beach Plaza Hotel, although out of town, is rapidly gaining favour, attracting a wealthy clientele seen in past years only at the Hotel de Paris, the Metropole and L'Hermitage. The Casino, opened in 1863 and designed by Charles Garnier, who was also the architect of the Paris Opera House, naturally survives, a perpetual lure for rich and impecunious alike. However, it is no longer unique, for there is also a casino at the Loews Hotel. In years past, the Casino Square was the scene of an annual 'Poseurs' Grand Prix', as flamboyant tourists in Ferraris, Maseratis and Lamborghinis paraded in the streets on the eve of the official race. Today the symbolism is a shade more subtle, but still the crowded area in front of the Hotel de Paris often contains around £500-worth of exotic machinery per square foot.

There are too many bars in Monte Carlo to count or remember, but if there is one which the Grand Prix has virtually immortalized, it must be the Chatham Bar, owned and run by Rosie and Jean-Louis Bernard. A refreshingly unsophisticated social landmark on the climb to the Casino Square, Rosie's Bar, as it is affectionately known, is one of Monaco's most enduring – and endearing – traditions. Rosie's is not a glamorous nightclub; it is essentially an all-day bar, characterized by a constant, easy-going bustle. Inside, the walls are lined with photographs of the drivers and other racing people who have returned time and again to this friendly oasis, its long slim bar always crowded with spectators, journalists and – when the race is over for another year – sailors from all over the world. It is not hard to imagine the outcry which attended a 1969 demolition order placed upon the Chatham Bar. The bar, it was decreed, would have to go in order to make way for a new road. Princess Grace and Prince Rainier were inundated with protest letters from as far away as Nihon University in Japan, the Caribbean and the United States. The British Automobile Racing Club and BBC commentator Raymond Baxter appealed on behalf of British motor sporting interests, and the Pretoria Motor Club also pleaded for the survival of this most cherished of trackside institutions. The House of Grimaldi listened and sympathized and, 20 years on, the crowds still flock to Rosie's Bar.

The social armada which engulfs the town for the Grand Prix is accompanied by a water-borne invasion of even more dazzling splendour. Despite an increase in the number of available berths, the port is still filled to capacity with yachts and cruisers of every description. The boats serve as floating hotels for drivers, sponsors and spectators and, now that an exclusive Formula 1 paddock has been established beyond La Rascasse, there is the added attraction of a grandstand view of the paddock for those whose yachts are moored near the Quai Antoine 1er. In fact, the reality of life for a Grand Prix yacht-dweller is often less idyllic than the dream, for the

Left: No Grand Prix paddock has such a spectacular setting – the Formula 1 teams set up on the harbour side, with the Royal Palace high on the hill above them. Boats moored alongside the Quai Antoine 1er accommodate drivers and sponsors during the race weekend.

Below: This helicopter shot, taken an hour before the start of the 1986 Grand Prix, is by Jean-Marie Moll, former bodyguard of Princess Grace. Moll's aerial pictures are used by the authorities of the Principality to check crowd management and safety facilities during the race weekend.

waters of the harbour are regularly disturbed by a Mediterranean swell, and more than one seasick enthusiast has been known to abandon a luxury yacht and stumble ashore in search of a hotel room with a stable horizontal bed!

From a promotional point of view, the use of a yacht as an operational base – a small private island, surrounded by water – offers obvious advantages over more conventional accommodation. There is less likelihood of guests or key personnel wandering off at inopportune moments, and it is easier to mount a comprehensive social programme if sponsors are located in one place. Certainly, these logistics helped TAG McLaren Marketing Services to organize a highly successful promotional venture when they hired the Cunard cruise ship *Sea Goddess 2* for the weekend of the 1988 Grand Prix and provided accommodation for 106 guests in 58 berths as well as a four-day programme of sophisticated social activities. As a footnote to this rather conspicuous exercise, it is worth pointing out that the hosts were able to repackage much of the accommodation for their associated sponsor companies to use for their own promotional needs, thereby ensuring that the major investment was virtually self-liquidated.

Alone amongst Grands Prix, Monaco generates a social ambiance of which the race itself is but the nucleus. As early as Friday evening, the Sporting Club on the beach is the venue for Marlboro's gala reception and dinner for the Grand Prix fraternity, the company's biggest single social event of the sporting year. On Sunday night, when the last magnum of victory champagne has been emptied over the track and the cars are back in their transporters, the teams and sponsors return to the Sporting Club for the celebration dinner organized by the Automobile Club de Monaco, culminating in a midnight firework display. The winning driver and team manager are the focus of attention at an event which invites comparison with the Wimbledon Ball as Grand Prix racing's most illustrious ceremonial occasion.

Exerting a benign yet intensely supportive influence over all these activities, His Serene Highness Prince Rainier III has long been the Monaco Grand Prix's staunchest advocate. His unswerving enthusiasm reflects the House of Grimaldi's 60 years of commitment to motor sport in the Principality. It is a royal patronage which succeeds in being at once munificent and yet discreet, and it bestows upon this great event a unifying authority of a kind granted to no other Grand Prix. The position of the royal box makes it an impossibly noisy platform from which to view the entire race, but Prince Rainier invariably opens the circuit in a locally-supplied Rolls-Royce and watches the first few laps, returning in time to present the trophy to the winner.

While Monaco is aggrandized by its Grand Prix, it is also disrupted by it, far more so than other more recently added street circuits on the Grand Prix itinerary, where it has been possible to minimize the civic and commercial inconvenience by locating the circuits – and race traffic – away from a central hub of essential services.

Within the uncompromising confines of Monte Carlo, this is plainly impossible. The circuit comprises streets which are normally busy with everyday traffic and provide the only access route between Monaco and the port of Monte Carlo. Since the Grand Prix 'carnival' lasts for four days, every possible provision has to be made for the continuation of routine business by those who are neither involved in the event nor interested in it. Thus, the traffic must be rerouted, often through streets not designed to cope with the increased volume, and extra police have to be drafted in to control the diversions. With typical Monegasque good humour, the police maintain a polite but efficient supervision throughout the long weekend.

Because the circuit roads are only 'borrowed' from the Principality's main network, the circuit is constantly sealed and unsealed to facilitate the movement of ordinary traffic. Access gates are sited at strategic points, and there is also an intricate maze of pathways channelling spectators to and from

Right: Sunday morning untimed practice, 1988, and Ayrton Senna's McLaren-Honda leads Gerhard Berger's Ferrari past the fashion boutiques on Massenet just before Casino Square. Below: With a flag-bedecked yacht in the background, Nelson Piquet (Lotus-Honda) leads Berger's Ferrari during the 1988 race.

their hotels. The Armco itself, like a huge Meccano set, is periodically unbolted and later reassembled. Minor gaps only may be opened between practice sessions, but when the day's competition is over, all the main access barriers are removed as soon as the last racing engine has been switched off. After Saturday's supporting Formula 3 race, the entire circuit is swiftly reopened to the public, then closed again early the following morning for the final build-up to the Grand Prix. Each section of Armco is numbered to indicate its position in the overall structure, and on Sunday evening the pieces are removed and stored, ready to be put back in the same slots next year.

Understandably, so much turmoil encourages a mixed reaction from the local population. Since they may be woken at 5.30am by the raucous bark of revving engines, the Monegasques are entitled to a degree of reservation. But while the Grand Prix has its local detractors, the mood is generally supportive. One of the main objectives in bringing the race to the town in the first place, in 1929, was to attract tourism, and there is no doubt that the sheer spectacle of the event has never ceased to draw vast crowds, and substantial revenue, into the Principality at a time when the peak Riviera tourist season has yet to begin. Suddenly the yacht berths, hotel rooms, restaurants, bars and shops are filled to overflowing with the influx of multinational visitors.

The hard core are dedicated motor racing enthusiasts, but many more come simply to savour the overpowering atmosphere of this unique and most festive of Grands Prix. Many of the race enthusiasts travel on package tours and though some of them may stay in hotels outside Monte Carlo, they still spend money in the bars and shops, where a motor racing theme features in most window displays at Grand Prix time; at the open-air cafes, especially those adjacent to the circuit along the road from Ste Devote to the chicane; and at the racewear and souvenir stalls lining the access roads. Far from being an economic obstruction, the Grand Prix generates its own unique and lucrative commercial impetus.

It is one of the great paradoxes of modern Grand Prix racing that, with such enormous sums of money pledged to the sport, drawn principally from television rights and sponsorship, few Grands Prix can ever hope to be self-liquidating. Nowhere is this more apparent than at Monaco, with its heavy burden of organizational expenses and its dearth of paying spectators. In recent years, the total estimated attendance at the Grand Prix has varied between 40,000 and 70,000, but as there are less than 20,000 grand-stand seats available, the bulk of the crowd watches from the sheer rock-face or from the balconies and roof-tops of trackside buildings.

The race they flock to see, and hear – for Monaco is a Grand Prix walled in by blocks of deafening, shattering noise – celebrates its 60th anniversary this year. It is not the oldest Grande Epreuve, but it is the most evocative and the most controversial. Current attitudes in international motor sport ensure that there will never be another race quite like it. In the shifting firmament of the Grand Prix constellation, it is still the brightest star.

One Man's Dream

There are older motor races than the Monaco Grand Prix but, with the possible exception of Le Mans, none that welcomes its aficionados with quite the same intoxicating cocktail of nostalgia, vibrant local colour and sheer cacophanous excitement. Monaco is the Grand Prix which every driver needs to win and every enthusiast wants to visit. It is the quintessential motor racing experience.

Although other towns have hosted 'round the houses' Grands Prix, seeking to emulate the success of Monaco's spring festival of motor sport, no venue has yet come close to reproducing the little Principality's richly charismatic spectacle. Monaco is unique, and one suspects that, by this distinction, it will outlive its imitators and survive subversive criticism.

Certainly, and understandably, the race has its detractors. Over the years, many drivers, while lamenting their inability to win at Monaco, have reviled the course for its claustrophobic design, its poverty of safe passing places, its bumpy surface, its ineradicable dangers and the debilitating effect on both man and machine. As a place to stage a motor race, it is impractical, horrendously expensive and grossly disruptive of normal commercial life. Yet, in this age of high-technology motor sport, forever questing after greater margins of safety and surer profits, the Monaco Grand Prix endures, a glittering and splendid anachronism.

For all that in recent years several street circuits have been added to the Grand Prix map, and still more are under consideration, it is extremely doubtful whether the idea of a Monaco Grand Prix, if freshly proposed in the 1980s, would have elicited anything other than hoots of derision from drivers, Monegasques and FISA alike. The birth of this particular legend arose from the dreams of one man who, apart from the sport's international governing body, the AIACR (International Association of Recognised Automobile Clubs), had only the local residents to convince.

He was Antony Noghes, the Director General of the Automobile Club de Monaco, who in 1928 caused a stir when he suggested a motor race through the narrow streets of Monte Carlo, the area which encompasses the resort segment of the Principality. To many, not least the AIACR (forerunner of today's FISA), it was a lunatic scheme. But with Noghes and his vision began the story of the Monaco Grand Prix.

In today's parlance, Antony Noghes was a 'high flier'. He was responsible for securing the Automobile Club de Monaco's entry into the AIACR, which was a great honour for the small Club, and one which would allow it to organize motor sporting events on its own territory. Noghes' next dream was to see the creation of a speed circuit using the streets of Monte Carlo. He sent a telegram to Prince Louis of Monaco at the Chateau de Marchois informing him of the admission of the Club to the AIACR, and duly impressed, in due course Prince Louis offered him his support for his motor racing idea.

During October 1928, Noghes could be seen wandering around the streets of Monte Carlo, mentally mapping out the configuration of the circuit he had in mind. He wanted to have his plan ready to be presented as a package to the AIACR as soon as he had gained the support of his colleagues at the Automobile Club de Monaco.

After much thought, he made public his proposal to run a race through the streets, and he obtained the essential support of the Club's President, his father Alexander Noghes, and Alexander Taffe, the Club's first Vice-President.

The Automobile Club de Monaco, which was derived from the Cycling and Automobile Sport Club, had a good pedigree, for in 1911 it had founded the Monte Carlo Rally, once the best known of international rallies. A race around the streets, however, was fraught with problems of both logistics and safety. Nevertheless, the House of Grimaldi was behind Noghes, for it could see the value of such a race, as the economy of the Principality relied upon tourism, as did all the fashionable resorts of the French Riviera.

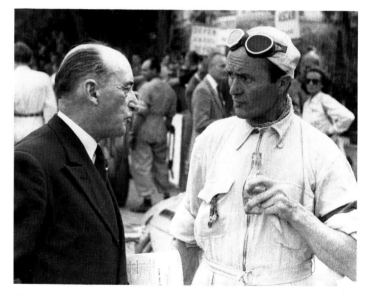

Elsewhere, early reaction to Noghes' proposals was hardly more sympathetic than it would be today. The Monegasques thought that it would be impossible to run a race in such a confined area, across tram-lines and between houses, and even the enlightened magazine *The Autocar* described as 'astonishing' and 'dangerous' the idea of organizing a Grand Prix in the switchback streets of the Principality. In contrast, support for the venture, and for the ideals of the Automobile Club de Monaco, came from Francois Dureste, an ex-racing driver and a new Monaco resident, who also gathered support from other drivers, and it was Club member Charles Bernasconi who eventually swayed the sceptics.

Rene Lyons, the administrator of the Societe des Bains de Mer, owners of the Casino at Monte Carlo, relieved the Automobile Club de Monaco of the financial worries of promoting such a controversial venture by underwriting any losses that might occur. Another Monaco resident, who was becoming well-known in motor racing circles, was Louis Chiron. Noghes recruited Chiron to advise him, which turned out to be a shrewd move as Chiron, after his active career as a driver of some celebrity, became associated with the project as the Club's Race Director.

After much planning, and finally winning the support of the local population, Antony Noghes had brought his great dream to the brink of realization. He spent a long time devising what he believed would be an ideal circuit. It passed the Port, ran along the quay, used the Boulevard Albert 1er, climbed the hill of Monte Carlo, passed round the Place de Casino, then took the downhill zig-zag past Monte Carlo station to return almost to sea level. Via the Boulevard Louis II and the Tir aux Pigeons tunnel, the course wound back to the quayside. Noghes could not avoid the tram-lined part of the circuit, nor the countless other hazards such as trees, kerbstones and lamp-posts. All movable obstacles had to be cleared, while the fixtures were protected by sandbags.

On April 14, 1929, Noghes' dream became a reality when the inaugural Grand Prix took place over 100 laps of the 1.97-mile circuit he had mapped out so enthusiastically. The winner was an Englishman driving under the pseudonym 'Williams', who was destined to drive a Bugatti in the Monaco Grand Prix on five occasions, either as a works driver or as a private entrant. He then passed into obscurity before emerging again during the Second World War in his adopted France, working as a member of the British 'Secret Army' until he was captured and subsequently shot by the Gestapo in 1943.

Monaco's first Grand Prix left Noghes a relieved but happy man because it had marked a good beginning, even though the event had been far from a financial success. Rene Lyons' agreement to fund and underwrite the first race was to prove fortuitous, for there would be a deficit of 610,000 francs. But Noghes had never conceived the Grand Prix as a self-financing project, and in all other respects his endeavours and foresight had been well rewarded.

In the years that followed, the Monaco Grand Prix assumed

CIRCUIT DE MONACO = 3180ᴹ

a mantle of glamour and importance which made the tiny Principality a natural focus of international attention, as prosperous enthusiasts flocked in their thousands from the surrounding countryside and from neighbouring nations to savour the drama, romance and prestige of this remarkable motor race. The success of Noghes' vision stood also as a testament to the faith of the House of Grimaldi, a strength and tradition which the present descendant of the family, His Serene Highness Prince Rainier III, steadfastly upholds to this day.

The Monaco Grand Prix is no mere elemental part of a series of World Championship events. It has acquired, and proudly proclaims, its own mystique, its own special place in motor sporting history.

The railway station was an important landmark on the Monaco circuit and gave its name to the picturesque downhill hairpin, where Jack Brabham (Brabham-Climax) and Richie Ginther (BRM) are shown hard at work during the 1964 Grand Prix.

When the railway was removed, the massive Loews Hotel took its place and provided a vantage point for guests to watch Stefan Johansson (Ferrari) and Ivan Capelli (March-Ford) during the 1987 race. The famous sea-front chicane has also been remodelled in recent years, as shown in the 1986 picture below.

Refining the Layout

It is no small tribute to the integrity of Antony Noghes' original concept that, 60 years after the inaugural race, the round-the-houses circuit today follows a course which differs only cosmetically from that used by the prewar Bugattis. No better place has been found for the 1929 start/finish line (notwithstanding the abortive experiment with a harbour-side location between 1955 and 1962) and the cars still climb steeply up into the town and return through the tunnel to the quayside. If, as is widely suggested, modern Grand Prix machinery has outgrown Noghes' invention, we can only be thankful that the vigilance and ingenuity of the Automobile Club de Monaco have miraculously contained that obsolescence.

While the Monte Carlo circuit of 1989 has evolved as a faithful replica of the original layout, it is not – and could never be – identical. Routine road improvement in the busy town, together with the stringent safety requirements of contemporary Grand Prix racing, have wrought constant changes in the 'furniture' of the circuit – often nothing more significant than the removal of a bollard or the flattening of a kerbstone – interspersed with occasional, more radical, redesign. The 'diary' which follows identifies most – and certainly the more significant – of the circuit modifications introduced up to the date of the 1988 race.

The first recorded improvement occurred in **1932**, when the tram tracks which had criss-crossed the circuit were taken up. The roads were then extensively resurfaced and the cobbled sections smoothed over. In **1935**, the chicane was altered for the first time, making it more acute. An interval of 20 years (though only five races) elapsed before the next change, an important but non-structural one. In **1955**, the start/finish line, which since 1929 had been sited on the landward side of the Boulevard Albert 1er, between the Gasworks hairpin and Ste Devote, was moved to the quayside stretch of track, so that the first corner after the start was the Gasworks hairpin.

In **1956**, after Ascari's dive into the harbour during the previous year's race, the chicane was made narrower and more sharply angled, with the aim of slowing cars at this point, only for it to be eased again in **1958**.

In time for the **1961** race, most of the straw bales around the circuit were removed and replaced with steel Armco barriers. In some areas, where head-on impact was considered possible, the bales were retained; for example, in front of the station and at the Gasworks hairpin. Also, the pit counters, which had hitherto faced the sea, were moved to the inland side of the tree-lined 'island'.

After the debacle of the 1962 start, the start/finish line for the **1963** event was returned almost to its original position between the Gasworks hairpin and Ste Devote. As a further safety measure, the familiar 3-2-3 starting grid was abandoned in favour of a 2-2 formation. By **1967**, the start/finish line had been moved nearer to Ste Devote, allowing more room for acceleration out of the hairpin.

The ideal design and position of the chicane has always been a contentious issue at Monaco. No other single physical feature of the circuit has been remodelled and transplanted in so many different locations over the years, to such inconclusive effect. In **1968**, in the aftermath of Bandini's 1967 accident, the chicane was moved down towards the Tabac and its angle sharpened, once again encouraging a slower entry.

For **1972**, the rudimentary and vulnerable pits were moved from beneath the trees of the Boulevard Albert 1er to a trackside position immediately after the old chicane. This meant that the working area was some considerable distance from the start/finish line, but the new location offered more working space for mechanics and pit crews and was considered much safer than alongside the 'dragstrip' before Ste Devote.

The original entry to the chicane now became the pit lane entrance, while the old chicane escape road was incorporated into the circuit, running down to a new chicane farther on. As the pits exit was blind for the drivers, their departure was controlled by a hand-operated traffic light. An underground garage near the start/finish straight was used as a Formula 1 paddock for cars which had formerly been accommodated in sundry garages throughout the town. Although the revised pit and paddock sites were quite well received by the teams, they were still very unsatisfactory logistically.

In **1973**, for the first time in Monaco's history, fundamental changes were made to the circuit, increasing the lap distance by some 150 yards. Major reconstruction on the lower quayside created a new, fairly narrow stretch of track around the new swimming pool, below the level of the original circuit. The extra loop left the old circuit at a left-hand bend after the Tabac, rejoining it at a redefined right-handed hairpin, now called La Rascasse, and preceded by a left-hand curve. This allowed the old road between the Tabac and the former Gasworks hairpin to be made into the pits area, offering better working facilities and a more direct view for the public. Access to the pits was via a right turn after La Rascasse, and the cars exited on to the circuit after the start/finish line, where lights controlled emerging traffic.

With the abandonment of the 1972 pits site (which had suited some teams but few spectators), the chicane was once

again returned closer to the hill following the exit from the tunnel. Extensive redevelopment was also apparent between Portier and the tunnel entrance, which was widened when the tunnel itself was rebuilt. The new structure was longer and had modernized internal lighting as well as natural light access on the seaboard side.

As part of a general road improvement programme in the town, the road at Ste Devote was resurfaced in **1975**, reducing the camber. This, of course, benefited the Grand Prix cars as well as the motoring population. Meanwhile, the Formula 1 paddock was moved to a more permanent position on the harbour front beyond La Rascasse.

In **1976**, in an attempt to reduce the number of accidents at Ste Devote, the fast right-hand bend was modified by the introduction of a large chicane, as described in the race report. Improvements were also made at La Rascasse, where the track was widened at the exit. Amid rumbles of disapproval from the purists, Louis Chiron's picturesque but hazardous practice of starting the race by standing in the road, dropping the national flag and scuttling aside, was discontinued in favour of starting lights. It was commonly felt that a set of light bulbs was a miserable substitute for Chiron's colourful ritual, but safety and efficiency held sway, and the enthusiast could at least console himself with the reflection that the timely intervention of technology had probably prevented the local hero from being run over!

The circuit as it appears today was finally formed in **1986**, when the chicane was squared off into a complex of more positive bends, further slowing the cars after the tunnel, and the exit from La Rascasse was redefined.

The true street circuit will always demand an enlightened compromise in the areas of safety and practicality. At Monaco, where a 70% increase in race speeds has been contained by intelligent management, it is history itself which argues for the survival and prosperity of the Monaco Grand Prix into the 1990s.

The Automobile Club de Monaco's official circuit map, below, confirms that the Grand Prix takes place on a course fundamentally similar to that which Antony Noghes conceived for the inaugural race in 1929, albeit with many cosmetic improvements. It remains one of the most exhausting tests for a Formula 1 driver, as indicated by Alain Prost's gear-change points on the map, right. Just to complete a Monaco Grand Prix is a considerable achievement by both driver and car, let alone to win one. Prost was first across the finishing line in 1984, 1985, 1986 and 1988.

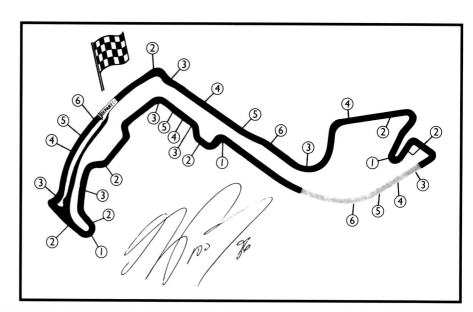

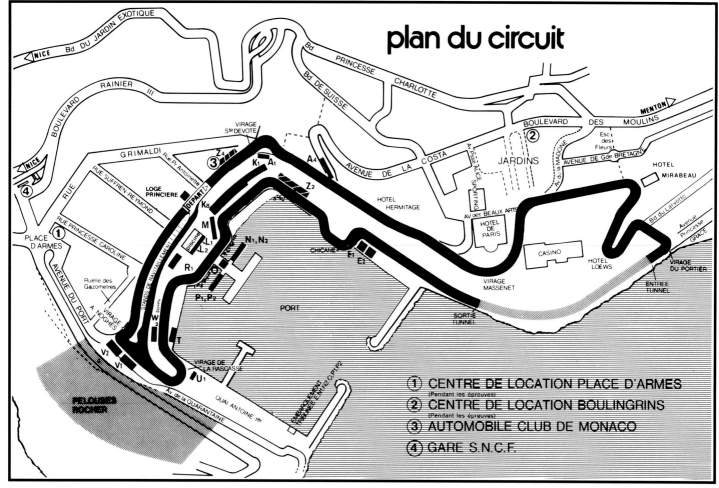

plan du circuit

① CENTRE DE LOCATION PLACE D'ARMES
(Pendant les épreuves)
② CENTRE DE LOCATION BOULINGRINS
(Pendant les épreuves)
③ AUTOMOBILE CLUB DE MONACO
④ GARE S.N.C.F.

In recent years the Monaco champion has been Alain Prost, left, whose hat-trick of Grand Prix wins was earned driving the Porsche-engined McLaren-TAG, although engine trouble broke the sequence in 1987, below.

1929

'Williams' Opens the Record Book

Under the patronage of His Serene Highness Prince Louis II, Antony Noghes' main advocate, the inaugural Automobile Grand Prix de Monaco attracted 23 entrants, from which 16 cars lined up for the start after the attrition of the trials (as practice sessions were then called), with the Alfa Romeo team considered to be the pre-race favourites. In bright sunshine, the enthusiastic Prince formally opened the circuit and the crowded buildings echoed to the roar of the departing pack as 15 cars – one being left stranded on the grid – set off on their 197-mile journey.

Despite the predictions, the race quickly developed into a battle between Rudolf Caracciola, in the huge 7.1-litre Mercedes-Benz, and the expatriate Englishman, William Grover, competing under the pseudonym 'Williams' in a 35B Bugatti.

After Marcel Lehoux had led initially in a 35C Bugatti, 'Williams' quickly moved ahead, while Caracciola worked his way through the field from near the back of the grid to become the English driver's main challenger within the first 10 laps. Thereafter, 'Williams' and Caracciola traded first place between routine pit stops until the German lost further time with a stop for tyres and slipped to third place, leaving 'Williams' to run out the winner by almost 78 seconds ahead of Emile Bouriano, of Belgium, in a 35C Bugatti, after almost four hours of racing. 'Williams' had averaged 49.83mph in an exhausting race from which only nine cars survived.

Making a start. The poster listed 19 entries, but 16 cars came to the start for the first Monaco Grand Prix, their grid positions decided by ballot. The only British entrant, 'Williams', driving a Bugatti, below, scored a notable victory.

PREMIER

GRAND PRIX AUTOMOBILE DE MONACO

organisé par

l'Automobile Club de Monaco

avec le concours

de l'International Sporting Club et du Journal *L'Auto*

DIMANCHE 14 AVRIL 1929

à 15 heures 30 précises

100 tours du Circuit soit 318 kilomètres

LISTE DES ENGAGÉS

ALLEMAGNE :	CARACCIOLA.........	Mercédès Benz
AUTRICHE ... :	STUCK	Austro Daimler
BELGIQUE ... :	BOURIANO	Bugatti
FRANCE ..... :	DAUVERGNE.........	Bugatti
	DORE	Licorne
	DREYFUS	Bugatti
	ETANCELIN	Bugatti
	LAMY	Bugatti
	G. PHILIPPE.........	Bugatti
	DE ROVIN	Delage
GRANDE-BRETAGNE... :	WILLIAMS	Bugatti
ITALIE........ :	GHERSI	Alfa Roméo
	PERROT..............	Alfa Roméo
	RIGAL	Alfa Roméo
	SANDRI	Maserati
	DE STERLICH	Maserati
	ZEHENDER............	Alfa Roméo
POLOGNE .... :	BYCHAWSKI..........	Bugatti
SUISSE....... :	LEPORI	Bugatti

1930

Bugatti
Clean Sweep

Run to the same free formula as the inaugural race, the 1930 Monaco Grand Prix was to prove a resounding success for Bugatti, whose cars finished the 100-lap race in the first six places.

Louis Chiron, whose name would soon become inextricably linked with the Monaco event, led the 17 starters away, chased by team-mates 'Williams' (William Grover, winner of the 1929 race) and Guy Bouriat. Chiron set a new lap record of 2min 13sec, which was shortly reduced to 2min 11sec by the flying Bouriat, whose progress was interrupted a lap later by an accident at the chicane. René Dreyfus, Philippe Etancelin, Juan Zanelli and Bouriat, who had recovered from his contretemps, challenged for the lead of a furious race until, on lap 83, Chiron made a 44-second pit stop, handing first place and eventual victory to Dreyfus, who crowned his triumph with a lap record of 2min 7sec, which would stand until 1932. Completing the course in 15 minutes less than the previous year's time, Dreyfus lapped all but the luckless Chiron, who followed him home in second place.

Compare the picture, below, of the first lap in 1931, with the rear view, bottom left, of the cars jockeying for position as they go up the hill past the Beau Rivage. Caracciola's big Mercedes SSK is about to overtake the Bugatti of Lehoux.

1931

Sweet Revenge for Chiron

Below: Tram-lines were a hazardous feature of the circuit until 1932. Right: A brace of Bugattis on the seafront in the afternoon sun, 1931, and bottom right, Dreyfus in the works Maserati leads Lehoux's Bugatti through Tabac.

Some 28 entries were received for the 3rd Monaco Grand Prix, including works Type 51 Bugattis for Chiron, Achille Varzi, Albert Divo and Bouriat, and 11 privately entered Bugattis, one of which belonged to the English aristocrat Lord Howe. Ranged against this formidable presence were three works Maseratis (one to be driven by 1930 winner Dreyfus) and cars from Mercedes, Alfa Romeo and Peugeot.

A large grid of 23 cars took the start, Dreyfus leading the field uphill from Ste Devote, tailed by the Bugatti of 'Williams', which assumed a short-lived lead before retiring. Varzi and Caracciola then harried Dreyfus until lap 7, when Varzi moved ahead. Behind them, the redoubtable Chiron was in relentless pursuit, equalling the lap record as Caracciola faltered and Luigi Fagioli, in the Maserati, mounted an assault in which he, too, equalled the lap record. Chiron, scenting victory before the people of his home town, swept into an unassail-able lead, the hard-charging Fagioli displac-ing Varzi to take second place, splitting the Bugatti ranks. Chiron, Fagioli and Varzi shared the fastest lap of 2min 7sec after their great battle.

1932

The Italian Challenge

For the first time at Monaco, a foreign challenge to the Bugatti supremacy seemed in prospect as a strong team of 2.3-litre 'Monza' Alfa Romeos lined up with the phalanx of Bugattis, and three works Maseratis further reinforced the Italian assault.

Chiron, 'Williams' and Lehoux, all in Bugattis, took an immediate lead, pursued by Arialdo Ruggeri's Maserati. Pressure from behind spurred Chiron to a new lap record as early as lap 6, while his team-mate Varzi was climbing steadily through the field to occupy third place. A threat to the all-conquering Bugattis now appeared in the form of Tazio Nuvolari's Alfa, the little Mantuan sweeping all before him as he charged into second place, only 5 seconds behind Chiron's Bugatti. Squeezed between Nuvolari and a back-marker, Chiron hit the sandbags at the chicane and was thrown from his car, fortunately without serious injury. The incident let Nuvolari into a lead he held to the finish, crossing the line less than 3 seconds ahead of Caracciola, also in an Alfa Romeo. With Fagioli's Maserati taking third place, the only crumb of consolation for the vanquished Bugatti team was a new lap record of 2min 2sec for Varzi.

1933

Incident and Accident

This was the last race to be run to the free formula which had hitherto allowed entrants carte blanche in the design of their cars, and it was the first Grand Prix for which starting grid positions were determined, not by drawing lots, but on the basis of recorded practice times. The new qualifying system inevitably resulted in a number of accidents, as drivers fought to outpace one another, and both Nuvolari and Caracciola were involved in practice crashes, the latter injuring himself too badly to race again that season.

Varzi's Bugatti started from pole position and was soon embroiled in a titanic duel with Nuvolari, who was to harry him throughout the race. Under constant attack, Varzi set a new lap record of 1min 59sec on his penultimate tour, thus becoming the first man to lap the Monaco circuit in under 2 minutes. Nuvolari over-revved his Alfa Romeo's engine on the 99th lap, and a subsequent fracas brought about his disqualification. Varzi, meanwhile, cruised to victory almost a lap ahead of Baconin Borzacchini's Alfa Romeo.

Louis Chiron led the 1932 race, but trying to squeeze past a back-marker at the chicane, a hub-cap clipped a sand-bag and his Bugatti rolled three times. He was thrown out but not seriously injured. The drawing below, by Bryan de Grineau, was commissioned after the 1933 race and shows the race-long duel between Nuvolari's Alfa (car 28) and Varzi's Bugatti (car 10).

By 1934 grid positions were determined by practice times, as today, but drivers raised their hands to indicate that their engines had started – the opposite of the modern procedure. Station hairpin seen from the outside during the 1934 race, below, with Etancelin's Maserati, in pursuit of the leader Chiron, about to lap Siena's Maserati and the Alfa Romeo of Count Trossi.

1934

A New Formula

As though to acknowledge that the concept of the Grande Epreuve was here to stay, the governing body of international motor sport sought to rationalize Grand Prix car design by introducing a 750-kilogram formula. Race eligibility depended upon the car weighing a maximum of 750kg, dry and without wheels, but as before, there was no restriction on engine size.

Carlo Trossi's Alfa Romeo was fastest in practice, and the Alfas started as firm favourites, with additional cars for Varzi, Chiron and Guy Moll. The race was a less desperate affair than the previous year's, being run at a slower average speed and with no improvement in the lap record. The Alfas of Moll and Chiron finished the course in command of the race, though a minute apart, and Moll recorded his first and only victory at Monaco, with Dreyfus third in the Bugatti, a lap behind. It was a notable success for the Italian team, but the Alfas' superiority, and a plague of pit stops amongst the other competitors, robbed the event of much of its excitement.

Lap 1 of the 1934 Grand Prix and Louis Chiron (Alfa Romeo) shows Rene Dreyfus (Bugatti) and Philippe Etancelin (Maserati) the way past the Hotel de Paris and through Casino Square.

1935

Three-Pointed Star Ascending

Newcomers to the Monaco entry list appeared in the formidable shape of three 3.99-litre W125 Mercedes-Benz, to be driven by Manfred von Brauchitsch, Caracciola and Fagioli in a team managed by the meticulous and charismatic Alfred Neubauer.

In practice, no-one could compete on equal terms with the enormous power of the Mercedes cars, and Caracciola set the fastest time, followed by von Brauchitsch and Fagioli. This was a remarkable performance, for the W125 was a difficult beast to control around the twisting streets of Monte Carlo.

Fagioli and Caracciola led from the start, while von Brauchitsch retired his car almost immediately. Fagioli broke the lap record on lap 6 and consolidated his lead, but Etancelin in the Maserati had passed Caracciola and kept the Mercedes at bay for six laps until brake problems forced him to slow. With the retirement of Caracciola, the Alfas of Dreyfus and Count Brivio moved into second and third places, but Fagioli, posting a new lap record of 1min 58.4sec, was uncatchable. To the dismay of the subdued crowd, no French car was among the first six finishers.

> **Roll of honour published after the 1935 race, above, shows the first seven Monaco Grand Prix winners. Luigi Fagioli's Mercedes, right, led the 1935 event from start to finish.**

MONACO

11 ET 13 AVRIL 1936

Louis Chiron was invited to join the Mercedes team for the 1936 race and was fastest in practice. Here he leads team-mate Caracciola, who was to win the race.

1936

German Offensive

Run in the rain for the first time, the 8th Monaco Grand Prix was notable for two other 'firsts' – the debut of the sensational V16 Auto Unions and the first appearance of a rear-engined Grand Prix car on the streets of Monte Carlo. A trio of Auto Unions for Hans Stuck, Bernd Rosemeyer and Varzi vied for supremacy with the Mercedes-Benz team, for whom Chiron had now been invited to drive.

With the circuit like a skating rink, 18 cars streamed away, led by Caracciola's Mercedes and Nuvolari's Alfa. Chiron, after an excellent practice lap which had won him pole position, lost control on a patch of oil, and in the ensuing melee Giuseppe Farina's Alfa, von Brauchitsch's Mercedes and three following cars became entangled. Rosemeyer's Auto Union spun, narrowly avoiding the chaos, and later Fagioli crashed his Mercedes at the chicane, leaving only Caracciola's leading W125 circulating out of the four Stuttgart entries. Rosemeyer, having escaped unscathed from the earlier accident, hit the wall at the Casino Square on lap 13 and retired, while Varzi and Stuck in the other Auto Unions drove on cautiously in second and third places, taking no chances in cars which were demonstrably unsuited to the treacherous track. After a superb drive in terrible conditions, Caracciola won for Mercedes, nearly 2 minutes ahead of Varzi.

1937

Mercedes Invincible

In this, the last prewar Monaco Grand Prix, the might of Mercedes-Benz was finally all-conquering. It was clear from the outset that the race would be dominated by the German teams, for the Mercedes of Caracciola, von Brauchitsch and Christian Kautz were shadowed by the Auto Unions of Rosemeyer, Stuck and Rudolf Hasse. They were the most powerful cars yet seen on the Monaco circuit, and the race was a convincing demonstration of their speed and strength, as a result of which the opposition was totally annihilated.

Caracciola in the Mercedes was fastest in practice and set a new lap record in the race of 1min 46.5sec, a staggering 11.9sec faster than Fagioli's record just two years earlier. Even the Auto Unions could not compete with the Stuttgart cars, which finished first, second and third, von Brauchitsch victorious in a record race time of 3hr 7min 23.9sec, which was to remain unbeaten until 1955. With Farina's Alfa Romeo the first non-German car home in sixth place, the Teutonic commitment, as war clouds gathered, could hardly have been more eloquently stated.

1948

First Postwar Win to Farina

The return of the Monaco Grand Prix after the War saw the 10th event of the series and a win for Giuseppe Farina, who received the trophy from Princess Ghyslaine, wife of Prince Louis II, and Prince Rainier. To the left is Antony Noghes, President of the Automobile Club of Monaco.

By 1948, the year of the first postwar Monaco Grand Prix, the classification 'Formula I' had come into being, specifying maximum engine capacities for Grand Prix cars of 1,500cc supercharged and 4,500cc unsupercharged.

After the ravages of war, the 21 entries were a necessarily random assortment of old and new machinery. Much favoured were the 4CLT Maseratis of Farina and Clémenté Bucci, while four other Maseratis were entered for Villoresi, Emanuel de Graffenried, Ascari and Nello Pagani. Still active 18 years after his first race appearance at Monaco, Chiron in the Talbot earned a place on the fifth row of the starting grid, though nearly 7 seconds slower than Farina in pole position.

At the end of the first of 100 laps, Villoresi led Farina, but by lap 4, with Villoresi and Ascari slowed by gearbox trouble, Farina led and Chiron was starting to climb through the field. On lap 46, Farina stopped for fuel and restarted, still in first place, ahead of Chiron and Jean-Pierre Wimille's Simca-Gordini. Wimille's race ended on lap 60 with a blown engine, but Chiron could not be dislodged from second place and completed the course on the same lap as the winner, a distinction achieved by no other runner.

1950

Easy Win for Fangio

1950 – a freak wave soaked the road at Tabac and caused this shambles on the first lap. Fangio's Alfa Romeo, to the right of the picture, somehow found a way through on his second lap and went on to victory. Below, Stirling Moss, on his first visit to Monaco, celebrates with his parents after winning the 500cc Formula 3 race. Pits scene, right, shows De Graffenried and Fangio with, to the right of picture, Trintignant and Bira.

For the first Monaco Grand Prix in the new World Championship series, 19 cars were assembled on the grid, headed by the Alfa Romeo of Juan-Manuel Fangio, whose best practice lap had been 2.6 seconds faster than that of team-mate Farina alongside him.

When the flag fell, Farina rushed into the lead with Fangio on his tail, but almost immediately, Fangio overtook and led Farina down to the Tabac, where the accident occurred which was to decimate the field and remove all prospect of a competitive race. Losing control of the Alfa on a sheet of sea water which had splashed over the harbour wall, Farina rebounded from the wall in front of the closely-grouped pack. Luigi Villoresi, running behind him, scraped through, as did Chiron in the Maserati, but as the following cars arrived on the scene they found Farina and Fagioli blocking the road and could not avoid cannoning into the stalled Alfas.

Only one driver – Franco Rol, in a Maserati – was injured in the pile-up, but 10 cars were eliminated, leaving scant opposition for the flying Fangio. For a while it seemed that the Ferraris of Villoresi and Alberto Ascari might make an impression on the leading Alfa, but their repeated stops for fuel, and the eventual retirement of Villoresi, dashed even this faint hope. Fangio finally cruised home a lap clear of Ascari after a race which had effectively ended on the first lap.

1952
Sports Car Diversion

In 1952 and 1953, the Drivers' World Championship was contested in the Formula 2 category. There was no single-seater Monaco Grand Prix in either year, but a 100-lap race for sports cars was run on June 2, 1952 and was won by the Ferrari of Vittorio Marzotto. Sadly, Luigi Fagioli, now aged 54, crashed in practice and died three weeks later. The relatively cumbersome sports-racing cars, with their all-enveloping bodywork, presented an incongruous spectacle on the narrow streets of the Principality, and the experiment was not repeated.

With Formula 1 dormant, the AC de Monaco decided to run the Grand Prix for sports cars in 1952. Up the hill to the Casino on the first lap, Stirling Moss's C-type Jaguar has already gone but Pierre Levegh's Talbot leads a gaggle of Ferraris and Aston Martins. Marzotto's Ferrari, car 96, won.

1955
Grand Prix d'Europe

After an interval of five years, 22 Grand Prix cars (their engines now restricted to 2,500cc unsupercharged) returned to the streets of Monte Carlo to fight for the 20 places on the starting grid. Much favoured were the Mercedes-Benz of Fangio, Stirling

44

Moss and Hans Herrmann, the first two drivers being allocated special short-wheelbase cars uniquely suited to the twisting circuit. The pair duly qualified for the front row, sandwiching Ascari's Lancia, but Herrmann crashed early in practice and his place was taken by André Simon.

Fangio, Eugenio Castellotti (Lancia) and Moss led from the start. Moss was soon past Castellotti, and the two Mercedes then began pulling away from the rest of the field, with the Lancias of Ascari and Castellotti battling with Jean Behra's Maserati for third place. However, the speed of the German cars was not matched by their reliability, and Fangio retired with a broken axle on lap 50, whereupon Moss inherited a handsome lead over Ascari, only to lose it 30 laps later when his engine failed.

On the same lap, Ascari, now in the lead, slid wide at the chicane and plummeted into the harbour in an immense cloud of steam. The Lancia sank to the bottom, but the shaken driver managed to scramble clear and swim to safety, although he would die a few days later while testing a car at Monza. Maurice Trintignant in the Ferrari, who had been lying third before misfortune struck Moss and Ascari, found himself suddenly elevated to the lead with only 19 laps remaining. Despite a strong bid by Castellotti, in second place, to close the gap, Trintignant sped to an unexpected victory in a race filled with drama and incident.

1956

Fine Victory for Moss

A compact field of 14 cars faced the starter, headed by the Lancia-Ferraris of Fangio and Castellotti, with Moss' 250F Maserati between them. Two other promising British drivers, Mike Hawthorn and Tony

Moss, Fangio and Collins – they were inter-related in the stories of the 1956 and 1957 Grands Prix. In 1956 Moss won well for Maserati, even after Collins, left, had handed over his Lancia-Ferrari to an unusually ragged Fangio. The following year, Mike Hawthorn explains to Collins how Moss had caused the pile-up at the chicane, as Fangio's Maserati sweeps by to victory, below.

Brooks, had been entered in BRMs, but engine problems forced the withdrawal of both cars before the race.

Moss jumped into an immediate lead, followed by Castellotti, Fangio and Harry Schell in a Vanwall. Yet again there was an opening-lap accident, caused by Fangio spinning at Ste Devote and running backwards downhill into the path of Castellotti, whom he had just passed, Peter Collins and Behra. These three slipped safely through, but Luigi Musso's Ferrari and Schell's Vanwall collided with the straw bales and retired. Fangio, meanwhile, had resumed the race in fifth place and set about the task of catching Moss in the lead. He relentlessly reeled in Castellotti, Behra and Collins, his other Lancia-Ferrari teammate, to lie second behind Moss until, on lap 32, he made another error of judgment and bent a wheel on the harbour wall. On lap 40 he stopped at the pits for a new wheel and handed his car over to Castellotti, whose own had expired on lap 15. Castellotti rejoined the race in fifth place.

On lap 54, when Moss was leading Collins by some 30 seconds, Fangio reappeared in the pit lane and Collins was called in to hand over his car to the Argentinian. Fangio set off in third place behind Behra's Maserati, which he rapidly overhauled, but even a brush with a back-marker did not disturb Moss' concentration, and he scored a popular and skilful victory.

1957

Fangio on Form

For this year's gruelling 105-lap race, there were 16 places on the grid and three different marques on the front rank – the Maserati of Fangio in pole position, the Lancia-Ferrari driven by Collins alongside him, and Moss' Vanwall third quickest on the outside.

Moss and Fangio hurtled side by side into the Gasworks hairpin, but as the leaders accelerated up into the town, Moss held the advantage over Fangio, with Collins in pursuit. By lap 2, Collins had passed Fangio to close on Moss, ready to bid for the lead. On lap 4, however, Moss entered the chicane too fast and ploughed into the barriers, hurling poles and sandbags in all directions. Collins was too close to the Vanwall to take avoiding action and crashed into the harbour barricades. Fangio, running third, scraped by, but Brooks, in the other Vanwall, braked on seeing the wreckage and was promptly struck astern by Hawthorn's Lancia-Ferrari, which rode up on top of Collins' stationary car, shedding a front wheel into the harbour.

Of the four damaged cars, only Brooks' was able to continue, and he set off in second place behind Fangio, a position he held to the finish. With three of the main contenders eliminated, Fangio dictated the race from the front. Gearbox trouble slowed the Maserati in the closing stages, allowing Brooks to gain ground, but 25.2 seconds separated the two as Fangio took the chequered flag.

1958

A Turning Tide

Slowly but inexorably, the competitive face of Formula 1 was assuming a very different perspective. Gone were the days of illustrious Italian marques trouncing a meagre opposition; British cars had finished second, fourth and sixth at Monaco in 1957, and among a strong entry list for the 1958 race were works teams from Vanwall, BRM, Lotus, Connaught and Cooper.

Serving due notice of intent, Brooks soon recorded a pole-position practice time in the Vanwall, with the somewhat under-powered but nimble Coventry Climax-engined Coopers also proving disturbingly fast around the tight circuit.

At the start, Roy Salvadori leapt into the lead in the works Cooper, only to be involved in the usual first-lap affray at the Gasworks hairpin. This let Behra's BRM into first place, followed by Brooks, Moss in another Vanwall and the Ferrari of Hawthorn, who was scything through the field, setting fastest lap as he passed Moss and closed on Brooks.

As so often at Monaco, mechanical attrition took a hand. All three Vanwalls retired, and Hawthorn stopped on the circuit with the Ferrari's fuel pump hanging loose. It was left to Trintignant, circulating consistently in Rob Walker's private Cooper, to improvise an unexpected but prophetic victory, the first ever for a rear-engined car at Monaco. The Ferraris of Musso and Collins, second and third, were the only continental cars in the first six at the end of this fastest Grand Prix to date.

Maurice Trintignant in Rob Walker's Cooper was a surprise winner in 1958. Left, he is being led by Behra's BRM, Brooks' Vanwall and Brabham's Cooper on the first lap. Jean Behra's Ferrari out-accelerates Moss' Cooper at the start in 1959, but it was Cooper number 24 driven by Jack Brabham that won. Note the shortened noses of the Ferraris – to avoid traffic jam damage at Monaco!

1959

First Win for Brabham

Sadly, after their heartening victory in the 1958 Constructors' Championship, the Vanwall team withdrew from competition because of Tony Vandervell's ill-health. Thus, British hopes rested once again with the Coopers, BRMs and a single qualifying Lotus, ranged against the Ferraris and a handful of Formula 2 cars.

With 24 cars competing for 16 places on the grid, practice was a hectic affair, Moss in the Rob Walker-entered Cooper finally snatching pole position from Behra's Ferrari and Jack Brabham's works Cooper. Seven rear-engined cars — nearly half the field — lined up for the start.

Behra led Moss and Brabham through the opening laps, with Phil Hill's Ferrari lying fourth. The tail-end Formula 2 race was abruptly terminated on lap 2 when Wolfgang von Trips spun and collected Cliff Allison and Bruce Halford. On lap 21, Moss found a way round Behra, shortly to be followed by Brabham, while the Ferrari

Jack Brabham, above, won his first Grand Prix at Monaco on the way to the 1959 World Championship. Cooper's Formula 1 success spelt the end of the front-engined Grand Prix car, and the American Scarabs that appeared in 1960, right, were too late and didn't qualify.

Jo Bonnier (BRM) led from the second row at the start in 1960, ahead of Brabham (Cooper) and Brooks (Cooper). At the end, though, it was masterful Moss who won the last 2½-litre Monaco Grand Prix in Rob Walker's Lotus 18. It was his and Walker's second Monaco win.

slowed with engine trouble. In fourth and fifth places, Brooks (Ferrari) and Schell (BRM) were locked in combat, and the race was further enlivened by Brabham spinning harmlessly at the Station hairpin and Phil Hill thumping the straw bales at the Casino, continuing with the Ferrari's tail deranged.

Keeping a cool head amid the drama, Moss consolidated his lead over Brabham. Brooks lay third, but his was a dogged and uncomfortable drive, for the heat and fumes in the enveloping cockpit were becoming unbearable. Then, just as victory seemed assured, Moss ground to a halt with a broken transmission, leaving Brabham out in front, 10 seconds ahead of the ailing Brooks. Brabham responded with a new lap record to seal his first Grand Prix victory.

1960

A Race of Attrition

Now that 16 starters had come to be regarded as the safe maximum for the tight Monaco circuit, practice sessions were frequently as exciting as the race itself as up to 24 cars – the number entered this year – fought for places on the grid. Unfortunately, the perils of this arrangement were high-

Success at his fingertips – Stirling Moss's 1961 win in the 'out-classed' Rob Walker Lotus was one of the Monaco classics. Anticipating a tough race against the Ferraris, Moss had the car's side-panels removed, keeping him cool and adding a psychological advantage.

lighted in first practice when Allison crashed heavily in the Ferrari and was seriously injured. When the dust settled, Moss was easily fastest at the wheel of Rob Walker's Lotus 18. Brabham, next to him in the Cooper, was a second slower, an appreciable deficit around this 1.95-mile circuit.

Jo Bonnier made a brilliant start in the rear-engined BRM, with Brabham and Moss behind him. With the BRM looking a serious contender at last, Bonnier led until lap 17, when Moss moved ahead, leaving the Swede to contest second place with Brabham, Phil Hill's Ferrari and a gaggle of pursuers. Retirements came thick and fast, and a shower of rain at quarter-distance greased the road and spaced out the field as spins took their toll. Brabham, who had taken the lead on lap 35, gyrated into the wall six laps later, letting Moss past once more, still tailed by Bonnier. On lap 60, Moss, with a commanding lead, made a brief pit stop to have a loose plug lead replaced, but it then took him only eight laps to catch and overtake the BRM, which was shortly to retire with broken rear suspension.

Moss pulled out a comfortable margin over Bruce McLaren's Cooper, but behind him a lunatic spectacle developed. With only four cars still running, drivers who had recently retired staggered back on to the track in stuttering, crabbing machinery, eager for the Championship points still at stake. Thus the race ended in dangerous farce.

1961

Moss: A Touch of Genius

If some races are destined to live long in the memory, this one will surely endure for ever. Right from the start it had all the ingredients of a classic Grand Prix: a strong entry list; the unknown quantity of a new Championship formula; and the prospect of a David-and-Goliath battle between the might of Ferrari and Moss in an under-powered private Lotus.

British vaccillation over the 1½-litre Formula 1 ensured that only Ferrari, who entered three cars, were really ready for this, the first Championship race under the new rules. Nonetheless, Moss, as ever at Monaco, outpaced everyone in practice, driving Rob Walker's Lotus fitted with a stopgap ex-F2 Coventry Climax engine.

Richie Ginther made a fine start from the middle of the front row in the new Tipo 156 Ferrari V6, Jim Clark and Moss giving chase in Lotuses. The American, with a power advantage of at least 30bhp over the Climax-engined cars, held on for 14 laps before being displaced by Moss as he mounted a sustained display of driving virtuosity. Bonnier's Porsche moved up to harry Moss as Ginther tired and fell back, but by lap 25 Bonnier was falling prey to the Ferraris of Phil Hill and Ginther in their pursuit of the leading Lotus. First Hill and then Ginther, advancing for his second attack, hounded Moss without respite, but on a circuit where skill and handling were at a premium, there was no denying Moss his triumph. He crossed the line 3.6 seconds ahead of Ginther after a superb drive.

1962

V8 v V6

Since the previous year's race, major development work on the two new British V8 engines, the Coventry Climax and the BRM, had restored the balance of power in Grand Prix racing, as BRM had demonstrated by winning the season's opening Grand Prix in Holland. It was therefore a more optimistic British contingent who arrived in Monaco for the 20th Grand Prix, although the absence of Stirling Moss, seriously injured at Goodwood, seemed particularly poignant. As in 1961, the five works teams were guaranteed two grid places each, leaving the remaining 11 entries to scrap for the other six positions. Clark in the works Lotus gained pole position, followed by Hill's BRM and McLaren's Cooper.

The traditional early carnage occurred only seconds after the start when Willy Mairesse, starting from the second row, forced his Ferrari through the narrow gap between Clark and Graham Hill, consequently arriving at the Gasworks hairpin impossibly fast and almost spinning in front of the pack. While Mairesse fumbled his way round the corner, Ginther's BRM, Trintignant's Lotus, Innes Ireland's Lotus, Trevor Taylor's Lotus and Dan Gurney's Porsche collided with the straw bales, Ginther, Trintignant and Gurney retiring immediately. This bizarre incident was tinged with tragedy, for a flying wheel from Ginther's car struck and killed a marshal standing nearby.

McLaren had made the best of the

Michael Hewett's first Monaco Grand Prix saw him in the thick of the first corner chaos – in the main picture Mairesse, who caused the accident, leads out of the Gasworks hairpin as Richie Ginther has a wheel from his BRM bounce over his head (far right). Lower left shows the rest of the field accelerating away, Trevor Taylor's Lotus with an up-turned nose. Graham Hill's BRM, inside Surtees' Lola-Climax, led the race, but the winner was Bruce McLaren, pictured below with his wife Pat.

diversion and was in the lead, soon to be passed by Hill's BRM. A strong challenge by Clark in the Lotus came to nought when he retired from second place with clutch failure. Hill held his lead over McLaren until lap 93, when the BRM expired and McLaren raced to the flag with Phil Hill's Ferrari filling his mirrors.

1963

BRM Benefit

In an effort to alleviate first-corner congestion, the organizers assembled the 15 starters on a two-by-two staggered grid, situated for the first time since 1952 on the opposite side of the track between the Gasworks hairpin and Ste Devote. Another change in qualifying rules meant that this year only five drivers had guaranteed starts – World Champions Brabham and the two Hills and past winners McLaren and Trintignant.

Clark put his Lotus on pole position, but it was the BRMs of Graham Hill and Ginther that led from the flag, with Clark and John Surtees' Ferrari following. By lap 17, Clark was in front, and Surtees began to press Ginther in an attempt to split the BRMs. He was past by lap 28 and closing on Hill, though it took him a further 29 laps to wrest second place from the BRM driver, who was able to regain his position a few laps later when the Ferrari slowed with falling oil pressure. Throughout all the excitement, Clark had maintained what appeared to be a secure lead, but Monaco's notorious appetite for transmissions now brought about his downfall. With 22 laps to go, the Scotsman helplessly engaged two gears at once approaching the Gasworks.

Hill now found himself back in the lead with his team-mate a respectful distance behind him. In the closing stages there was drama, as Surtees made a determined bid to catch McLaren in third place. The task was too much, but Surtees' final inspired lap of 1min 34.5sec was a new record.

Previous pages show Monaco pictured from the Jardin Exotique in 1963. Understeering Formula Juniors at the Station hairpin, left, include 1961 and 1962 Junior race winner Peter Arundell, leading, and 1963 winner Richard Attwood, third. In the Grand Prix, Graham Hill (BRM) and Jim Clark (Lotus-Climax) fought for the lead, below. Monaco was the only Grand Prix victory that eluded Jim Clark, right, during his racing career.

1963 – previous year's winner Bruce McLaren (Cooper-Climax), left, finished third behind the two BRMs. Below, Jim Clark led the race until three-quarter distance, but retired with transmission failure. Right, Innes Ireland (BRP Lotus-BRM) chases the pack into Casino Square.

Dicing in the dark – 1963 Juniors in the old tunnel, replaced in 1973. Above, John Surtees in the Ferrari passed Ginther's BRM, but fell behind again when oil pressure faded. Towards the end of the race he made a determined but unsuccessful bid for third place, top right.

1963 was the first of Graham Hill's famous five victories at Monaco. Far left, he is waving the trophy after this narrow win from team-mate Richie Ginther, but in 1964, left, there was a margin of a lap in the BRM 1-2.

1964

BRM 1-2 – Again

In many respects, this was a race which bore an uncanny resemblance to the one preceding it. Once again, Clark was fastest in practice; he ran strongly in the race, only to retire with mechanical problems near the end, much as in '63; and for the second successive year the BRM team, led by Graham Hill, finished first and second.

Clark made a tremendous start to complete the opening lap well clear of Brabham (now in a car of his own manufacture), Hill, Gurney in the other Brabham, Surtees' Ferrari and Ginther's BRM. These five were inseparable for many laps, though no-one could offer a challenge to Clark, who steadily increased his lead. Eventually Gurney took the initiative and jumped from fourth to second, 6 seconds behind Clark's Lotus. Surtees retired the Ferrari with gearbox trouble and McLaren, lying sixth, withdrew soon afterwards, to be followed into the paddock by Brabham on lap 30. As ever, Monaco was proving to be a severe test of machinery.

By one-third distance, Clark led Hill by 10 seconds, but a first-lap contact with the bales had broken the Lotus' anti-roll bar mounting and the bar lay askew, trailing behind the car. A black flag seemed imminent, but Colin Chapman called his driver in to have the remains of the bar removed, Clark rejoining the race in third place. The new leader was Gurney in the surviving Brabham, but Hill's BRM was about to take over, setting a new lap record in the process. Once in front, Hill

began to pull away, despite an ominously smoking engine, and when Gurney's gearbox failed, the leader strove to fend off Clark's advancing Lotus. Then, on lap 92, Clark faded with no oil pressure and Hill was out on his own with Ginther a distant second.

Top left, Richie Ginther, three times second at Monaco, shares a joke with *Motor Sport*'s Denis Jenkinson. Jim Clark, far left, once again led the race, but retired with mechanical trouble. Brabham, above, also retired. Previous Monaco winners Juan-Manuel Fangio and Stirling Moss, re-united, left.

1965

Classic Hill

At a circuit where he was rapidly becoming as popular and successful as Moss had been in the early '60s, Graham Hill was partnered this year by the very promising Jackie Stewart. The BRMs looked quick and clean in practice, and Hill took pole position, while Stewart was third fastest.

The two BRMs made the best of the start, with the Ferraris of Lorenzo Bandini and Surtees third and fourth. Hill and Stewart wasted no time in opening a gap behind them, and the possibility of a runaway win for the Bourne team seemed likely. This race, however, was destined to be anything but processional. On lap 25, Hill emerged from the tunnel to find Bob Anderson's disabled Brabham crawling into the chicane right in the BRM's path. Hill braked violently and shot up the escape road, then scrambled out of the car and pushed it back on to the circuit, rejoining the race in fifth place.

Stewart, who had taken over the lead, spun down to fourth place on lap 30 and waved his team-mate by a few laps later. Within 20 laps of his excursion, Hill was into third place and catching the two Ferraris. By lap 53, he had dived past Surtees to lie second, and lap 65 saw him take the lead from Bandini at the Gasworks hairpin after a mesmeric drive. After such breathless excitement, even the sight of Paul Hawkins launching his Lotus over the straw bales and into the harbour seemed unremarkable. Hawkins surfaced wet and shocked, while Hill came home a hero.

Bruce McLaren (Cooper-Climax) leads Richard Attwood (Parnell Lotus-BRM) past the old Mirabeau Hotel, above, while John Surtees lines the Ferrari up to overtake back-markers going into the Station hairpin. Note the brave and/or foolhardy photographer in the centre of the escape road!

1966

Formula for Success?

True to tradition, the dawn of a new 3-litre Grand Prix formula rose over a racing fraternity universally unprepared for it. There were new engines in the offing, notably an intriguing H16 from BRM and the outline of a much simpler V8 as a joint venture between Ford and Cosworth, but the 16 cars that lined up for the 24th Monaco Grand Prix were essentially interim models powered either by old undersized engines or by units adapted from sports-racing categories.

Yet again, Clark's Lotus set fastest practice time on a circuit which had never been lucky for him. As if to show that in this respect the new formula would change nothing, the works Lotus jammed in first gear when the flag dropped and was last away. Surtees' Ferrari led Stewart's BRM, these two keeping close company for 13 laps until the Ferrari's differential failed and Stewart was in front. While the Scot extended his lead, Bandini defended second place in the other Ferrari against Jochen Rindt's Cooper-Maserati and Hill's BRM.

In typical style, Clark was carving his way through the field after his abysmal start, and on lap 61 he took second place from Graham Hill, only to suffer the immediate collapse of his rear suspension. Just seven cars now remained, and some of them were distinctly unhealthy. Stewart drove serenely on, virtually unchallenged, with Bandini settling for second place and the small consolation of fastest lap.

A new star emerges – Jackie Stewart, driving a 2-litre 'Tasman' BRM, had a clear win in the first Monaco Grand Prix run to the new 3-litre Formula 1. Also typical of the 'interim' cars of the time are the two private entries below, the BRM V8-engined Lotus of Mike Spence and the similarly-powered Rob Walker Brabham driven by Jo Siffert.

Full 3-litre cars, heralded as 'The Return of Power', came from Ferrari (with a sports car-derived V12), Brabham (Repco V8 based on a Buick) and Cooper (using a Maserati V12 engine). John Surtees in the Ferrari V12, above, led Stewart and the race in the early stages. Left: While Jack Brabham had the Repco V8, team-mate Denny Hulme used a four-cylinder Coventry Climax engine to hold off Jochen Rindt's works Cooper-Maserati in the early laps.

1967

A Race in Shadow

An assortment of interim and new machinery appeared on the grid for the 25th Monaco Grand Prix. The start/finish line had now been moved up towards Ste Devote to allow a better sprint to the chequered flag after the hairpin. Brabham's Brabham-Repco was fastest in practice, ahead of Bandini, runner-up in the two previous Monaco GPs, driving the purposeful-looking V12 Ferrari.

Bandini leapt into the lead at the start, followed by Brabham, whose engine burst dramatically after only a few hundred yards, spraying oil all over the road. Fortunately, the field managed to avoid the slick, although Clark's Lotus slid off on lap 2 on a slippery mixture of oil and cement, Clark rejoining at the tail end. A tremendous tussle was taking place at the front where Hulme's Brabham and Bandini's Ferrari were taking turns in the lead, closely

Start and finish – Race Director and 1931 Monaco Grand Prix winner Louis Chiron horrified competing drivers with his flamboyance and unpredictability with the starting flag. Denny Hulme, in his Brabham, car 9, only just managed to avoid him at the start of the 1967 race, but was the first to receive his enthusiastic wave of the chequered flag, below. Car 18 on the starting grid is the ill-fated Ferrari of Lorenzo Bandini.

followed by Stewart in the BRM, but when Stewart retired with transmission failure on lap 15, Hulme was able to contain the charging Bandini and extend his lead.

After half-distance, Bandini, tired but determined, began to reduce Hulme's lead again, bringing it down to 9 seconds. He then seemed to lose concentration, the interval steadily increased to 20 seconds, and on lap 82 he misjudged his entry to the chicane and clipped the inside barrier. Destabilized, the Ferrari careered across the track and mounted the straw bales, turning over in a pillar of flame. The car was eventually hooked upright and the poor driver extricated, but he was dreadfully burned and died in hospital three days later. Hulme went on to win his first Grand Prix by a lap, but the glum faces on the podium told us there was little to celebrate.

olygraphite TOTA

OWEN RACING ORGANISATION **4**

Above left, Hulme, Bandini and Stewart raise dust at the chicane on lap 2. The cement had been laid after Jack Brabham's engine expired and deposited oil on the racing line. Left, John Surtees (Honda) leads Jo Siffert (Cooper-Maserati) past the Hotel de Paris. Jackie Stewart was unable to repeat his 1966 win with the 2-litre BRM, above, but Graham Hill in the BRM-engined Lotus 33 and Chris Amon (Ferrari V12), right, finished in second and third places behind Hulme's Brabham.

Success and tragedy – Denny Hulme, far left, with one hand poised as the other winds on opposite lock, scored a fine win in the 1967 race which was marred by Lorenzo Bandini's fatal accident. In practice, below left, the Italian put his Ferrari on the front row of the grid. The picture, left, shows the initial impact with the straw bales at the exit of the chicane.

A happy Denny Hulme, pictured during practice in 1967, seems to say that he senses the opportunity for his first Grand Prix win. He finished a lap clear of the rest of the field, but as he stood on the royal balcony with the winner's trophy his delight was tempered by Bandini's accident. The traditional gala dinner on the Sunday evening was cancelled.

1968

Cosworth's First Monaco

Mindful of Bandini's accident the year before, the organizers had moved the chicane nearer the Tabac corner and made its angle more acute so that the cars passed through at a slower speed. This added about a second to lap times, and the race distance was reduced to 80 laps for the first time.

On the front row of the grid, Graham Hill in the very striking wedge-shaped Lotus 49, resplendent in its new Gold Leaf livery, occupied pole position, flanked by the Tyrrell-entered Matra of Johnny Servoz-Gavin, whose speed had surprised everyone. Both cars were powered by the already highly successful Cosworth-Ford V8 engine, which had first appeared in 1967, albeit too late to race at Monaco.

It was Servoz-Gavin, fast but wild, who led for the first three laps, with Hill's Lotus and Surtees' V12 Honda giving chase. Hill took the lead on lap 4, after the Matra had side-swiped a kerb, breaking the suspension. Also missing were McLaren's McLaren and Jackie Oliver's Lotus, both embedded in the guardrails. Jo Siffert, in Rob Walker's Lotus, moved up to press Hill, while Surtees was under attack from Rindt's Brabham, a threat which dissolved on lap 9 when Rindt crashed outside the Mirabeau Hotel. Surtees and Siffert proceeded to argue over second place, but both were out with transmission failures before quarter-distance, when only five cars were still running – Hill, chased by Richard Attwood in the BRM, then Hulme's

McLaren and Ludovico Scarfiotti and Lucien Bianchi in Cooper-BRMs.

The drive of the race now came from Attwood, making a rare but memorable appearance in a Grand Prix car. With a brilliant fastest lap of 1min 28.1sec on lap 76, he closed to within 2.2 seconds of Hill, who held him off to win his fourth Monaco Grand Prix.

John Surtees' years with Honda were frustrating. He was very directly involved in the team's management and car preparation, as can be seen from his spanner work watched by Honda engineer Nakamura and Race Director Chiron, opposite. On the first lap of the 1968 race, above, he leads Jochen Rindt's Brabham downhill from the old Mirabeau Hotel. The race saw Richard Attwood's finest Grand Prix performance in a one-off drive in a works BRM, left. Denny Hulme's McLaren-Ford, far left, eventually finished fifth after a pit stop.

1969

Hill Makes Five

Of the 16 starters in this year's race, 11 were powered by the ubiquitous Cosworth-Ford V8. That so many teams had a common, dependable power unit to rely upon was perhaps fortunate, for technical confusion reigned in first practice when an impromptu ban on certain kinds of wings and aerofoils eventually resulted in the cancellation of the first day's times. Once the regulations had been clarified, second practice gathered momentum, and Stewart in the Ken Tyrrell-entered Matra-Ford set fastest time ahead of Chris Amon in the Ferrari.

Paul Frère, the new Race Director, released the field, and Stewart and Amon set off at a blistering pace, with Hill in the Lotus keeping station at a safe distance. Brabham and Surtees crashed in the tunnel, and Amon retired shortly afterwards with differential failure, handing Stewart a generous lead over Hill. Two laps later, Stewart was out with a snapped drive-shaft, and Hill, driving with the impeccable calm of a Monaco veteran, once again found himself in the lead at Monte Carlo, needing only to keep going to take a record fifth win. Piers Courage, in the Brabham entered by Frank Williams, put in a determined effort to secure second place, and his 57th lap in 1min 25.8sec set a new circuit record.

Wings had reached new heights and sizes by the time for practice in 1969. McLaren, left, and Ickx (Brabham), left below, showed off their bi-planes for the last time; they were banned after the first session. Jackie Stewart, below, disappointment showing in his face as the Matra slows with a broken universal joint and Graham Hill sweeps past to take the lead. Hill, right, was the master of all he surveyed at Monaco in 1969.

Left: John Surtees swings the BRM round the Station hairpin shortly before colliding with Jack Brabham at the entrance to the tunnel, whence Brabham emerged on three wheels, below left. The BRM was later joined by other race casualties on the pavement, as winner Hill continued to speed by, below. Right, noted sports car specialist Vic Elford had the slowest car in the race (Colin Crabbe's Cooper-Maserati), but finished seventh.

Surprisingly, everyone went quicker after the big wings had been banned following the first practice session in 1969. Graham Hill's Lotus 49B, left, ran without rear aerofoil assistance in qualifying, but received a makeshift spoiler-cum-engine cover for the race. Fastest qualifier was Jackie Stewart in the Matra MS80-Ford, pictured above leading the second Lotus, driven by Richard Attwood in place of Jochen Rindt, injured in the Spanish Grand Prix. He added fourth place to Graham Hill's win, to the delight of Lotus chief Colin Chapman, right, with mechanics Eddie Dennis and Leo Wybrott.

1970

Last Minute Rindt

Before the start – a subdued Jochen Rindt, left, and a happy Jack Brabham. The smiles were reversed at the finish… Practice casualties, below, included Rindt, with a blown engine in his Lotus, who came to rest alongside Chris Amon, quietly having a cigarette while waiting for his crashed March to be recovered.

Throughout practice Stewart, driving Ken Tyrrell's March-Ford, was the man to beat. He was fastest in all three sessions and shared the front row of the grid with Amon's works March. Some 22 entries had contested the 16 starting places, and the race started with Graham Hill, the previous year's winner, perched ignominiously on the back of the grid in a Lotus borrowed from the works team after his own Walker-entered car had been shunted.

Stewart led Amon away from the start and began building up a useful lead over the New Zealander, while Brabham kept close company in third place. The lead changed on lap 27 as Stewart dived for the pits to have a faltering engine investigated, and Brabham, having disposed of Amon, took over at the head of the race. Stewart rejoined two laps down, but the problem had not been cured, and he finally retired on lap 58.

Towards half-distance the race was revitalized by a sudden charge from Rindt in the works Lotus. He stormed into third place on lap 40 and inherited second on lap 61 when Amon's March dropped out with suspension failure. Thus, with 19 laps remaining, Rindt, treating the crowd to a thrilling display of controlled aggression, began relentlessly to eat into Brabham's 13-second lead until he was catching him at 2 seconds a lap. As the two cars set off on their last lap, Rindt was crowding Brabham's mirrors, holding the Lotus on opposite lock over Monaco's crests and

It's over – Brabham's crumpled car limps past the line to finish second, while a surprised and delighted Rindt made his way to the podium and the winner's trophy presented by Prince Rainier, accompanied by Princess Grace and daughters Caroline, right, and Stephanie.

humps, while Brabham, with fading brakes and increasing fatigue, fought desperately to keep his attacker at bay. At the very last corner, the infamous Gasworks hairpin, the Brabham's wheels locked, sending the car into the barriers. Rindt was past in a red-and-gold blur to snatch a sensational victory.

Last lap, below, and Rindt flies – two-wheeling round Casino Square in a final desperate attempt to get to terms with Brabham. It was a record-breaking lap – and he won the race! Chris Amon, in the works STP March, right, ran second but retired.

1971

Stewart All the Way

The sun doesn't always shine at Monaco – Graham Hill, now a Brabham driver, walks back along the circuit after the first practice for the 1971 race had been rained-off.

For this race, yet another – and much simpler – qualifying method was adopted. The 23 entrants were instructed to fight it out for fastest times. No-one would have a guaranteed start, and the quickest 18 would form the grid.

Ken Tyrrell had entered two of the Ford V8-engined cars bearing his own name for Stewart and Francois Cevert. The Tyrrell was the latest of the Grand Prix 'kit cars', but it is doubtful whether its apparent superiority throughout the weekend owed as much to design excellence as to Stewart's masterful driving. A remarkable 1.2 seconds faster than Jacky Ickx, alongside him in the Ferrari, Stewart's pole time boded ill for all his adversaries.

From a grid for some reason 'reversed', so that pole position was on the inside, nearest the pits, Stewart seized an immediate lead, followed by Siffert's BRM and Ickx's Ferrari. In a race which was neither closely fought nor dramatic, there was little to watch but the indomitable Stewart, gradually extending his lead with consummate ease. Ronnie Peterson in the March added spice to the later laps by passing Ickx and Siffert for second place, but he could not catch the leader, who set a new lap record on his unchallenged run to the chequered flag.

Louis Chiron presents the Formula I drivers to Prince Rainier and Princess Grace. From the left: Cevert, Hulme, Amon, Fittipaldi, Ickx, Regazzoni (behind Chiron), Beltoise, Stewart, Pescarolo, Gethin, Stommelen. Pictured right, Jacky Ickx, who shared the front row of the grid with Stewart, and sheer delight showing on Helen Stewart's face after Jackie's perfect race.

Practice for the 1971 race was ruled by the weather. At the end of the final session, Jackie Stewart eases Tyrrell 003 through the damp streets. Earlier he had set a pole position time that was more than a second faster than the rest of the field. This dominance was to carry over to the race. While Stewart made it look easy, Ronnie Peterson got everyone's attention with a stirring drive in the odd-looking March 711, right, to second place.

1972

No Overtaking

The first wet Monaco Grand Prix since 1936 was a miserable, rather pointless affair, controlled at a pedestrian pace by the only two drivers who could see where they were going. With overtaking manoeuvres impossibly dangerous on the streaming track, this was essentially a ragged procession of dimly discernible fish-tailing cars.

Extensive alterations had been made to the circuit for the '72 race – see separate description – these being aimed at improving safety standards and working conditions for the teams. In view of the former objective, it was strange, and not entirely popular, that 25 cars were allowed to start. Only the first day's practice was of any account, as Saturday was wet. Emerson Fittipaldi in the JPS Lotus 72 was fastest, taking pole position next to Ickx in the Ferrari.

The track was virtually awash as the huge field slithered away, led by Jean-Pierre Beltoise in the V12 BRM, who had timed his start perfectly from the second row. The Ferraris of Ickx and Clay Regazzoni followed, but Beltoise, with the advantage of a clear view, pulled away at a second a lap. Even Ickx, acknowledged master of wet-weather racing, could make no impression on the BRM. The leading order remained constant for most of the race, though Regazzoni finally lost the Ferrari on lap 52, one of many who came to grief.

The two flexible V12s in the BRM and Ferrari powered Beltoise and Ickx safely home in a race which neither drivers nor spectators could possibly have enjoyed.

Two Formula 3 cars emerge from the only dry place on Sunday afternoon! In the 1972 Grand Prix, below, Francois Cevert (Tyrrell-Ford) heads Jacky Ickx (Ferrari) as they splash through the Station hairpin. Ickx finished second, but Cevert was classified 18th and last finisher.

Dry spell in first practice as Denny Hulme (McLaren-Ford) gets inside Dave Walker (Lotus-Ford) going into the Gasworks hairpin, below, and Ronnie Peterson gets crossed-up through the Station hairpin in the small and light F2-based March 721X, right. In the lottery of wet conditions in Sunday's race, none of these three was to feature.

First and only Grand Prix win for the French driver Jean-Pierre Beltoise turned out to be BRM's last. His P160 had started from the second row, after a good qualifying time in dry practice, below, and Beltoise gained the all-important advantage at the start. Nearest challenger was acknowledged wet-weather specialist Jacky Ickx, right, who held on to second place throughout. Just seeing where you were going was difficult enough; below right, Chris Amon (Matra-Simca) looks anxiously across to see if Graham Hill (Brabham-Ford) will let him through at the Station hairpin.

1973

Monaco Facelift

Since the previous year's race, the circuit had undergone further considerable modification. The redefinition of corners and a completely new length of track on the quayside had added nearly 150 yards to the lap, and early practice times suggested that the revised layout was some 5 seconds slower and probably harder still on brakes and transmissions.

Once again, it was Stewart in the Tyrrell-Ford who dominated practice. In brilliant sunshine, a blessed relief after the monsoon conditions of '72, 25 starters lined up, headed by Stewart and the JPS Lotus of Peterson. Cevert, Stewart's team-mate, burst through from the second row to lead the field round lap 1, but his moment of glory was short-lived as he hit a kerb and relinquished the lead to Peterson. Regazzoni (BRM) and Stewart were second and third, but a sudden change of fortunes occurred as early as lap 8 with the retirement of Regazzoni and the slow strangulation of Peterson's engine with fuel-feed problems.

For the remaining 70 laps of the 78-lap race Stewart held a modest but comfortable lead over Fittipaldi's JPS. The inevitable catalogue of mechanical disasters gradually decimated the field, and only nine cars were still running at the finish. Fittipaldi took full advantage of the emptying track to gain ground on the Tyrrell, setting fastest lap in the process, but Stewart was unperturbed and crossed the line 1.3 seconds ahead. Just as in 1972, he had never looked like losing.

Emerson Fittipaldi, left, presented Stewart with his closest challenge, quickly closing the gap in the final laps. Brother Wilson (Brabham-Ford) had run in third place behind Fittipaldi the Younger; in the picture below he leads Chris Amon in the Tecno. Right: From the Shadow (Jack Oliver's, alongside Niki Lauda's BRM) to the setting sun out of the chicane.

1974

Peterson in Charge

An enormous entry of 28 cars arrived to compete for the 25 starting places, no less than 23 of them powered by the remarkable Cosworth-Ford V8 engine. With this power unit now such an indispensable feature of Grand Prix racing, it was perhaps ironical that the front row of the grid for this particular race was occupied by two flat-12-engined cars, the Ferraris of Niki Lauda and Regazzoni. Ferrari had not won at Monaco since 1955, but the hordes of Italian supporters who flock across the border each spring surely believed that, this year, the red cars would triumph once again.

From the start, Lauda and Regazzoni gave them cause for optimism, surging into Ste Devote ahead of Peterson's Lotus, Jean-Pierre Jarier's Shadow and the rest of the pack. For a few moments it looked like a clean start, but then Hulme's McLaren ran into Beltoise's BRM, completely blocking the road and triggering a chain reaction of collisions among the following cars. Beltoise, Hulme, Brian Redman, Carlos Pace, Arturo Merzario, Tim Schenken and Vittorio Brambilla – more than a quarter of the field – were eliminated, either on the spot or after limping round to the pits.

While the wreckage was cleared, the two Ferraris commanded the race, Regazzoni leading Lauda. A further spate of minor accidents depleted the field to 13 cars by lap 12, and Peterson, who had earlier moved up to third place, was clawing his way back from sixth after an

Opposite: Ronnie Peterson was the star of Monaco, 1974, driving the four-years old Lotus 72 to its first win round Monte Carlo. Contented before the race, he listened to Colin Chapman's advice, while afterwards he drank the bubbly with his wife Barbro. Ferrari had found new form in 1974 with the driving team of Niki Lauda, left, and Clay Regazzoni, above. These two dominated practice and the early part of the race, but Lauda's engine failed and Regazzoni spun down to fourth place. Graham Hill, above left, looked pensive in the pit road before the race. This time the five-times winner would only finish seventh in his Lola.

incident with Carlos Reutemann's Brabham. Peterson's charge became the highlight of the race, as the Ferrari effort faltered. Regazzoni spun down the field, Lauda's engine coughed and died, and Peterson finally found his form as he raced on to his first win at Monaco.

1975

Forza Ferrari!

In the constant search for improved safety within the uncompromising confines of the Monaco circuit, the organizers had reverted to an 18-car grid, arranged for the first time in staggered pairs. There were 26 applicants for the 18 places, and fewer practice sessions than usual this year. Lauda in the Ferrari had little difficulty in setting fastest time, but perhaps the most commendable effort was that of Tom Pryce, second fastest in the UOP Shadow on his first appearance at Monaco.

It was raining as the cars made their way up the hill, led by Lauda and Jarier. Leaving the chicane, Jarier hit the barriers and Peterson took over second place. Between laps 17 and 26, with the track drying fast, the order was confused by a succession of pit stops as drivers came in to change their grooved tyres for slicks. This activity injected a certain interest into the race, but it made no difference to the lead, Lauda coming in on lap 24 and rejoining without losing his position. Behind him, Fittipaldi's McLaren and Pace's Brabham held an advantage over Peterson, but Pryce, after his fine practice performance, left the road at half-distance.

The early rain and the tyre stops had slowed the race considerably, making it impossible for the leaders to complete the stipulated 78 laps within the 2-hour time limit. Therefore, the distance was hastily reduced to 75 laps, and Lauda, who had led from start to finish, brought Ferrari their first Monaco win for 20 years.

Previous page: The 1975 race was started in rain. Lauda (Ferrari) led, as he did at the finish. Niki Lauda, right, took pole position, too, but when Graham Hill, far right, checked the lap times with his wife Bette he realized that he hadn't qualified for his last Monaco Grand Prix. Jody Scheckter drove a stirring race in the Tyrrell, below, using all the road and a bit extra . . . .

When the sun came out, leader Lauda, left, was soon into the pits to change on to slick tyres. He scored Ferrari's first win at Monaco since 1955. Second, less than 3 seconds behind at the finish, was Emerson Fittipaldi (McLaren-Ford), below.

1976
More Track,
More Cylinders,
More Wheels

In the aftermath of the big accident at Ste Devote in '75, a very tight chicane, almost akin to a roundabout, had been installed at this, the first corner after the start line. The general opinion was that the new chicane was certainly clumsy and probably more dangerous than the original corner whose hazards it was designed to mitigate. The total circuit length was now a fraction over 2 miles.

As in 1975, it was the Ferraris of Lauda and Regazzoni which dominated practice, though it was interesting that Lauda's pole time of 1min 29.65sec was over 3 seconds slower than the previous year when Ste Devote had been, by Monaco standards, a fast corner. Of particular note was the speed of the two six-wheeled Tyrrells driven by Patrick Depailler and Jody Scheckter, which handled superbly on this tortuous course.

Responding to lights instead of a flag for the first time at Monaco, the 20 cars took off behind Lauda's Ferrari. When they emerged from the sanitized Ste Devote there were only 18 of them as Alan Jones' Surtees and Reutemann's Brabham had collided. So much for improved safety. Lauda took control of the race, the 12-cylinder Ferrari looking and sounding magnificent as it circulated unchallenged. In his wake, the nimble Tyrrells were busy wiping smiles from the sceptics' faces as Scheckter and Depailler outran and out-classed the other Cosworth-Ford runners on their way to second and third places.

Down from Loews, formerly the Station hairpin, and a mid-field line-up of Jarier (Shadow-Ford), Mass (McLaren-Ford), Hunt (McLaren-Ford), Pace (Brabham-Alfa Romeo), Amon (Ensign-Ford), Nilsson (Lotus-Ford) and Pryce (Shadow-Ford). Clay Regazzoni, right, was second fastest in practice and Patrick Depailler, in the six-wheeled Tyrrell, below, made fastest lap and had a long dice with Regazzoni for third place.

Six wheels were not enough to save Depailler from this lurid slide out of Casino Square during practice, but the unusual Tyrrells impressed with their speed and agility. As in 1975, Niki Lauda had everything under control with a flag-to-flag victory. In the picture right, he is about to lap Pace's Brabham and has Tom Pryce (Shadow-Ford) behind him.

1977

Wolf in Full Cry

In a terrific drive, Jody Scheckter, below, led from start to finish in the still-new Wolf WR1, set fastest lap and never put a wheel wrong, despite constant pressure. He is airborne out of Casino Square, right, and over the moon about winning the Grand Prix of his adopted home, bottom.

Though the circuit was unchanged, there were some unfamiliar sights on the starting grid for the 1977 race – new cars, new sponsors and, most interesting of all, a new, dramatically improved WR1 Wolf from Walter Wolf Racing, Scheckter at the wheel. Apart from the Wolf, which qualified second fastest, the most spectacular performers in practice were the flat-12 Alfa Romeo-engined Brabhams of John Watson and Hans Stuck, the torque curve of the Alfa 12 perfectly suited to the low-gear acceleration demands of Monaco's slow corners.

From pole position, Watson tucked in behind Scheckter as the field of 20 departed. For what seemed like the first time in living memory, every car completed the first lap unscathed. Watson hounded Scheckter mercilessly, but to no avail, and by lap 30 the gap was widening as gearbox trouble slowed the Brabham to the extent that Watson began falling into the clutches of Lauda's third-place Ferrari. On lap 46, fumbling for gears, Watson took to the escape road at the chicane, and four laps later he was out for good, stalled with a seized gearbox at Ste Devote.

Lauda, now second, tried valiantly to catch Scheckter in the closing laps, failing by less than a second. After a flawless, intelligent drive, Schecketer brought the Wolf across the line to win his 'home' Grand Prix and give Cosworth and Ford the 100th Grand Prix victory for the amazing DFV engine.

Popular Swedes, alas no more. 1977 was to be the last time that Gunnar Nilsson, left, raced at Monaco – he died of cancer the following year. A couple of weeks after Monaco, Nilsson scored his first and only Grand Prix win in Belgium. Ronnie Peterson, right, was one of the 'greats' of 1970s motor racing. A natural talent, there was one win at Monaco amongst his 10 Grand Prix victories. He died following a start-line accident in the 1978 Italian Grand Prix.

Left, lap 1 into Mirabeau, and Lauda (Ferrari) in sixth place leads Depailler (Tyrrell-Ford), Hunt and Mass (McLaren-Fords) and the rest of the 20-strong field. James Hunt, right, ran fifth before retiring, but McLaren team-mate Jochen Mass finished fourth after a furious dice with Mario Andretti's JPS Lotus, below.

Left, Depailler's six-wheeled Tyrrell P34 chases Nilsson's Lotus down into Portier. Ronnie Peterson, right, had qualified his Tyrrell well, but was the first retirement of the race. Note the P34's side 'windows' to enable the driver to place the front wheels accurately; very necessary at Monaco. John Watson, below, put the Brabham-Alfa on pole, while Niki Lauda, bottom, was Scheckter's closest race rival.

1978

Dependable Depailler

Well-deserved win for Patrick Depailler, who made the most of the agility of the Tyrrell 008 to get well clear of the field. Below, he rounds Rascasse in the closing laps. It was the Frenchman's first Grand Prix win.

Before the race, history – and Ken Tyrrell – told us that Monaco wins are seldom achieved from behind the second row of the grid, such are the overtaking problems around this twisting and congested circuit. With his cars on the third and seventh rows after final practice, Tyrrell was at best philosophical about his chances of repeating the team's past successes here. Reutemann in the Ferrari vied with Watson in the Brabham-Alfa Romeo for fastest practice time, pole position finally going to the Argentinian.

This year, 20 cars took the start and, as Reutemann fumbled for a suitable gear, Watson and Depailler's Tyrrell flashed past him to lead the field into the first corner. Disaster befell Ferrari fortunes almost at once for, braking into Ste Devote, Reutemann banged wheels with Lauda's Brabham and punctured the Ferrari's left rear tyre. Lauda was able to continue in third place, a position he was to hold until lap 46, when he made a pit stop for two new tyres – and, it might have appeared, an injection of adrenalin which would set the race alight in its closing stages.

Watson's lead lasted 38 laps, Depailler and Lauda rushing past him when he took to the escape road at the chicane. Eight laps later, as Lauda left the pits in sixth place with fresh tyres, Depailler had increased his lead and Watson was about to be overwhelmed by the hard-charging trio of Gilles Villeneuve's Ferrari, Scheckter's Wolf and Peterson's Lotus. The Ferrari and the Lotus

Mario Andretti was to become World Champion in 1978, but at Monaco his JPS Lotus 78 let him down. In the picture below he leads Scheckter's Wolf and JPS team-mate Peterson through Mirabeau; their dice, for fourth place, lasted for 30 laps, but only Scheckter was running strongly at the end.

were soon to disappear, Villeneuve crashing spectacularly and Peterson retiring with a broken gearbox, but Scheckter hung on in third place. He could do nothing, however, to save himself from Lauda, driving like a man possessed after his pit stop, lapping even faster than he had managed in practice in his efforts to catch the Tyrrell. In the end, the Austrian had to settle for second, but it was an honourable failure.

High expectations – on the warm-up lap, above, Andretti, fourth on the grid, leads race winner Depailler up the hill from Ste Devote. In pole position was Carlos Reutemann's Ferrari, left, shown powering through the tunnel. Monaco 1978 gave little pleasure to Lotus team-mates Andretti and Peterson, above right, or Gilles Villeneuve, shown with a customary handful of opposite lock; the Canadian Ferrari driver crashed on lap 62. John Watson (Brabham-Alfa), below, led the first half of the race until a brake problem took him into the chicane escape road, letting Depailler through.

121

1979

Ferrari Foremost

Exactly 50 years after the inaugural Monaco Grand Prix, 20 cars lined up on the starting grid, headed by the Ferraris of Scheckter (winner in the Wolf in 1977) and Villeneuve. In a quite different sense, the two cars at the rear of the grid, the V6 Renaults of René Arnoux and Jean-Pierre Jabouille, were as noteworthy as those at the front, for this was the first appearance at Monaco of a turbo-engined Grand Prix car and, historically, the turbo Renaults and their ilk would not languish at the back for long.

For the present, though, the flat-12 Ferrari was probably best suited of all the current cars to the Monaco circuit. Having dominated practice, Scheckter and Villeneuve threatened to do the same in the race, leading by the end of lap 1 and pulling away from the rest of the field, with Lauda's Brabham in third place. The prospect of a challenge from Lauda was frustrated by Didier Pironi who, coming from fifth place in the Tyrrell, nudged Depailler's Ligier out of fourth position and then attacked Lauda on lap 22, tangling wheels with the Brabham and putting both cars into the barriers and out of contention.

On lap 54, when a Ferrari 1-2 seemed inevitable, Villeneuve suddenly came to a halt with a broken transmission. Scheckter, 17 seconds ahead of Regazzoni in the Williams, entered the final quarter of the race with the green-and-white FW07 gradually filling his mirrors; once again, the scene was set for a breathtaking climax to the Monaco Grand Prix. With 10 laps to go,

Second win for Jody Scheckter, this time for Ferrari, above. Lauda's Brabham-Alfa Romeo held third place at the head of a typical Monaco procession, left, but was pushed off and into retirement by Pironi. Opposite, the Lotuses, now Martini-sponsored, were not well suited to Monaco in 1979. Andretti, top, was an early retirement, while Carlos Reutemann overcame a catalogue of problems to finish third.

Regazzoni had reduced his deficit to 8 seconds and, as they began the final lap, the two cars were nose-to-tail, Regazzoni dodging and weaving as he struggled to find a way past the Ferrari. But Scheckter held his line and took the flag less than half a second clear of the Williams in the closest ever finish at Monaco.

123

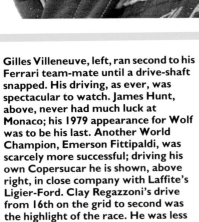

Gilles Villeneuve, left, ran second to his Ferrari team-mate until a drive-shaft snapped. His driving, as ever, was spectacular to watch. James Hunt, above, never had much luck at Monaco; his 1979 appearance for Wolf was to be his last. Another World Champion, Emerson Fittipaldi, was scarcely more successful; driving his own Copersucar he is shown, above right, in close company with Laffite's Ligier-Ford. Clay Regazzoni's drive from 16th on the grid to second was the highlight of the race. He was less than half a second behind Scheckter's Ferrari at the finish.

Contrasts – Lauda leads the Ligiers out of Mirabeau in 1979, while Neil Corner shows what it was like in 1937 with the Mercedes W125 in a historic race to celebrate the 50th anniversary of the Grand Prix. Appropriately, Louis Chiron, below, was united with a Bugatti like the one he drove to victory in 1931.

Jody Scheckter felt at home in Monaco, having moved to an apartment there in the mid-1970s. Work, when the Grand Prix came to town, was no more than a scooter ride away, as he explains to Niki Lauda, right. Compare the scene with the picture opposite as Carlos Reutemann's Lotus crests the hump in Casino Square in front of the Hotel de Paris.

1980

First Win for Williams

Even at slow circuits like Monaco, the writing was on the wall for the supremacy of the Ford V8 engine in Grand Prix racing, and this was to be the last year in which a turbo-powered car did not feature prominently in the results.

In practice, the 'home team' of Ligier, with cars for Pironi and Jacques Laffite, were strongly favoured. Though hardly elegant, the Ligiers were purposeful and fast, and Pironi took pole position, while Laffite, never one to take practice too seriously, occupied fifth place on the grid.

When the lights turned green, Pironi sprinted into the lead, followed by the two Williams of Jones and Reutemann. As the cars filed into Ste Devote, the mid-field runners fell victim to yet another spectacular first-lap accident. After clashing wheels with Bruno Giacomelli's Alfa Romeo, Derek Daly's Tyrrell was catapulted high into the air, crashing down on top of his team-mate, Jarier. With cars, either intact or fragmented, dropping out of the sky all around him, Alain Prost in the McLaren could not avoid the melée, and his was the fourth car to be eliminated before a lap had been run.

For the first third of the race, Pironi and Jones fought a spirited battle for the lead, with Reutemann and Laffite third and fourth. The pattern was broken on lap 25 when Jones retired with gearbox failure, allowing Reutemann into second place. Perhaps remembering Pironi's imprudent driving the year before, Reutemann

The exit from Ste Devote was reduced in width for the 1980 race and as 20 cars lined up for it after the start the inevitable happened. Derek Daly (Tyrrell-Ford) rode up on to a back wheel of Giacomelli's Alfa Romeo, pirouetted in the air and crashed down on top of team-mate Jean-Pierre Jarier, above. Alain Prost's McLaren (car 8) was also eliminated in the resulting melee. Miraculously, no-one was hurt.

decided not to risk a direct challenge and instead settled down to follow the Ligier, playing a waiting game. Sure enough, on lap 55 Pironi hit the barriers at the Mirabeau when the Ligier jumped out of gear and Reutemann was through, to run unhindered to the chequered flag.

Two masters of Monaco, Jackie Stewart and Stirling Moss, were there to present the event for American TV. They reported on a decisive win for Carlos Reutemann, below, driving a Williams, after pole position man Didier Pironi, bottom, had crashed into a barrier when leading for Ligier. Practice picture, right, shows Bruno Giacomelli's Alfa Romeo in the tunnel. Another disappointing race for Mario Andretti in the Lotus 81, being passed by Jan Lammers in the ATS, below right.

1981

Turbo Triumph

Of the 20 cars facing the starter, four were powered by 1½-litre turbocharged engines. Renault had brought turbo cars for Prost and Arnoux, and Ferrari appeared with new turbo engines for Villeneuve and Pironi. The Ferrari was not the most agile performer around the tight circuit, but a combination of sheer power and Villeneuve's natural forcefulness were sufficient to put the car in second place on the grid, next to Nelson Piquet's pole position Brabham. Nigel Mansell in a Lotus gave new heart to British interests by setting third fastest time.

A minor fire in the part of the Loews Hotel which had been built over the tunnel resulted in gallons of water pouring on to the road inside the tunnel shortly before the scheduled starting time. But after a delayed start the race began with Piquet, Villeneuve and Mansell settling into a lead which reflected their grid order. Behind them, Reutemann, in the Williams, was harrying Mansell's Lotus, and an altercation on lap 14 unfortunately put Reutemann into the pits and Mansell out of the race. Jones, in the other Williams, thus inherited third place and soon scrambled past Villeneuve to lie second.

As Piquet and Jones moved up to lap the back-markers, both were to encounter trouble. Seeing Jones drawing ever nearer in the traffic, Piquet lost concentration at the Tabac and hit the barriers on his 54th lap. Jones was into the lead, but the Williams was stuttering with fuel-feed

Gilles Villeneuve was out on his own at the end of the race, right, and on the limit throughout, in the turbo 1½-litre Ferrari left. He was ahead on the warm-up lap, too, left above, but Nelson Piquet's Brabham was on pole and led until an accident on lap 54.

problems, and a quick stop to take on fuel so reduced the Australian's advantage that Villeneuve's Ferrari was able to wipe it out completely on lap 72 and sweep into an unassailable lead.

John Watson (McLaren MP4-Ford) locks over for the Loews hairpin, left, with Jacques Laffite's Ligier-Matra in pursuit. Practice group, above, shows Chico Serra (Fittipaldi), who didn't qualify, ahead of Elio De Angelis (Lotus), who was sixth fastest, and Rene Arnoux in the Renault RE26B turbo. Neither were to finish the race on Sunday, but Gilles Villeneuve, right, was there to score the first win for a turbocharged car on a circuit which had seemed to be the least suitable for these ultra-powerful 'all or nothing' machines.

1982

The Winner? Who, Me?

Slowly but surely, turbocharged engine development was making an impression at Monaco. This year saw three turbo-powered cars on the first three rows of the grid – two Renaults and a Ferrari – and one of the Renaults, driven by Arnoux, was in pole position, the first time a turbo car had been fastest in practice at Monaco. Back on the seventh row, Piquet's Brabham-BMW was also turbo-powered.

At the start, Arnoux took an immediate lead, followed by Giacomelli in the Alfa Romeo and Prost in the second Renault. Prost's turbo power soon thrust him past the Alfa, and for 15 laps the crowds were treated to an all-French display of turbo potential as the two Renaults headed the field. The demonstration came to an end on lap 15, Arnoux spinning at the swimming pool and retiring with a dead engine. Prost took over the lead, chased by Riccardo Patrese's Brabham-Ford, Pironi's turbo Ferrari and Andrea de Cesaris in the second Alfa Romeo.

In a race which seemed doomed to mediocrity, the four leaders circulated in unchanging order for 59 rather tedious laps. Then the unexpected – which, paradoxically, may almost be regarded as commonplace at Monaco – happened, and the complexion of the race changed completely, and repeatedly, in the last three laps. A rain shower greased the track and Prost, caught unawares, lost the Renault at the chicane, letting Patrese into the lead. Moments later, Patrese spun and

Renaults had looked like winners in 1982, with Rene Arnoux, above, starting from pole position and leading the race before he spun, leaving team-mate Alain Prost in the lead. Prost went off when light rain fell in the closing stages. On the first lap, right, he led Pironi's Ferrari (eventually second) and Andrea de Cesaris (Alfa Romeo – classified third) through Casino Square.

restarted, but not before Pironi had passed him, only to have the Ferrari's engine die in the tunnel and de Cesaris take his place at the front. A disconsolate Patrese drove round to the finishing line – to be told that de Cesaris' Alfa had run out of fuel seconds after Pironi's demise. Patrese, confused but delighted, became one of Grand Prix racing's more extraordinary winners by default.

Andrea de Cesaris, leading Rosberg, left, and trailing Mansell, above, ran a hard race, but the engine in his Alfa Romeo lost power in the closing laps and the car coasted to a halt on that extraordinary final lap.

Keke Rosberg had been to Monaco twice before, but had not qualified, so his first race on this most famous of Grand Prix circuits was in his World Championship year with Williams. He spent 30 laps chasing de Cesaris, but broke the car's suspension against a kerb when the Alfa slowed. While team-mate Patrese scored a surprise victory, Nelson Piquet was much less happy in the turbo Brabham-BMW which Rosberg is passing, below.

So near but so far – Prost, in the tunnel, left, on his way to what seemed certain victory, and at the chicane, below, the site of his accident with four laps to go. Though not running at the finish, he was classified seventh.

Ferrari and Talbot-Lago head a gaggle of historic racing cars. Races and demonstrations of old cars, often with the celebrities who drove them in their heyday, became a regular and popular feature of the Monaco race weekend.

1983

Slick Decision

Not for the first time, the weather was to play a vital part in the outcome of the Monaco Grand Prix. Official practice to decide the 20 grid positions was scheduled for Thursday and Saturday, but the circuit was too wet during the second day for anyone to improve upon Thursday's times. Sadly, this meant that the McLarens, who had run into trouble in the first session, had no hope of qualifying.

On race day, the cars lined up on a circuit patchily wet from earlier rain. Easily fastest in the dry, Prost and Arnoux, in the turbo-engined Renault and Ferrari respectively, headed the grid in cars shod with 'wet' tyres, gambling on the probability of more rain, while the scene behind them was one of seething indecision as drivers and team managers scratched their heads and stared at the sky. But boldly, Keke Rosberg, fifth fastest in the Williams, chose 'slicks' and gambled on a dry race.

As the field took off, Rosberg shadowed Prost and passed him into Ste Devote at the end of the first lap. Within a handful of laps, cars on 'wets' were swooping into the pits for dry rubber, while Rosberg and Laffite in the two Williams led by a comfortable margin on the drying track. This situation prevailed until lap 54, when Laffite retired with gearbox failure, relinquishing second place to Piquet's Brabham. Piquet tried all he knew to catch Rosberg, setting fastest lap on his 69th tour, but time lost changing tyres was irretrievable. Rosberg won by 18 seconds.

Left, as the field streams down towards Mirabeau on the first lap, Nigel Mansell (Lotus-Ford number 12) elbowed his way past Chico Serra (Arrows-Ford number 30) on the pavement. He got away with that, but a few corners later a similar manoeuvre with Michele Alboreto's Tyrrell-Ford put both of them out of the race. Right and below, Alain Prost put the Renault on pole position, but led only on the first lap of the race. He finished third.

Left, Marc Surer (Arrows-Ford) knows that Derek Warwick (Toleman-Hart) is there, but couldn't prevent the collision that put them both out on lap 50. Rene Arnoux, below, was second fastest in practice and Nelson Piquet, bottom, second in the race. Jacques Laffite, right, had gearbox trouble when running second to his Williams partner Rosberg who, below, takes to the kerb to pass a group of back-markers led by Eddie Cheever's Renault.

1984

Red Light to Red Flag

The 20-car starting grid for the 42nd Monaco Grand Prix told its own story. Turbocharged engines powered 19 cars, and just one normally-aspirated car – Stefan Bellof's Tyrrell, slowest in practice – clung precariously to the back of the grid, its Ford V8 engine finally outpaced by the enormous power of the turbos. In pole position, Prost's McLaren with the TAG Porsche engine sat confidently alongside Mansell's Lotus-Renault. Prost's time of 1min 22.661sec was the fastest anyone had ever lapped at Monaco.

Sheer speed, however, was far from the drivers' minds as they moved into position for the start. Monaco was cloaked in cloud. Firemen hosed the road in the tunnel to make it as streaming wet as the rest of the circuit. Success today would depend upon concentration and car control as drivers forgot about blinding speed and peered through blinding spray.

Prost and Mansell tip-toed through Ste Devote, some of the field following in their tracks, others – like Derek Warwick, Patrick Tambay and de Cesaris – smacking the barriers for good. Risking everything, Mansell passed the McLaren on lap 10 to hold a tenuous lead, but it was to be short-lived. On lap 15, climbing towards the Casino, the Lotus slid wide on a slippery white line, slamming into the Armco, and Mansell spun to a stop moments later. Prost regained the lead, but Ayrton Senna in the Hart-engined Toleman, driving brilliantly in the downpour, was reeling him in. Bellof,

Not the sun-soaked Cote d'Azur! Left, Patrese (Alfa Romeo) leads Alboreto (Ferrari) and Senna (Toleman-Hart) through Rascasse. Magnificent shot, above, shows Mansell's vain struggle to maintain control of the turbo Renault-powered Lotus. Mansell, right, lost the lead when he struck a guard-rail. Team-mate Elio De Angelis, far right, finished sixth.

the only non-turbo runner, was also turning heads, chasing Senna relentlessly.

In the hopeless conditions, a major accident seemed inevitable so, on lap 31, Race Director Jacky Ickx cried 'Enough', and the red flag went out. Prost was still ahead, but Senna had closed to within sight of him and was closer still by the time the field slithered to a crawl on lap 32.

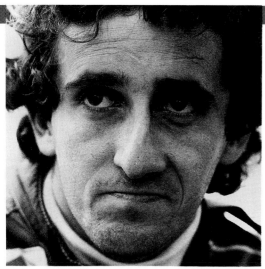

Alain Prost, left, didn't relish the prospect of a monsoon Monaco, but came through ahead. Ayrton Senna, right, was superb, and looked a likely winner in his Toleman-Hart until the race was stopped. Over the page, a practice picture of Elio de Angelis just millimetres from the guard-rail at 160mph, near the top of the hill before the Casino. Historic race, below, run earlier in the dry, was solely for Bugattis.

1985

Prost Again

Second win a row for Alain Prost driving the TAG Porsche-powered McLaren, below, who kept clear of the spectacular accident at Ste Devote on the 17th lap, right, involving Nelson Piquet's Brabham-BMW and the Alfa Romeo of Riccardo Patrese.

Seven different marques in the first eight places on the grid, with less than a second covering their times – the scene appeared set for a closely-fought race. Senna's Lotus in pole position was flanked by Mansell's Williams, less than a tenth of a second slower, while Martin Brundle in the venerable Tyrrell-Ford languished on the ninth row with the only non-turbo engine to qualify.

At the start, the front-runners set off in grid order, Senna ahead of Mansell and Michele Alboreto's Ferrari. The traditional first-corner accident this year claimed Gerhard Berger's Arrows, Tambay's Renault and Stefan Johansson's Ferrari, Ste Devote maintaining its reputation as one of the most expensive corners in Grand Prix racing. Alboreto, meanwhile, was pressing Mansell and took him on lap 2, immediately setting his sights on Senna. As Mansell's car developed brake trouble, Prost caught and passed him in the McLaren, and by lap 13 Alboreto and Prost were first and second, for Senna's engine had expired.

Farther down the field, Patrese, in the Alfa Romeo, led an exasperated queue of applicants for his position, including Piquet, Laffite and Teo Fabi, nose-to-tail. On lap 17, entering Ste Devote, Piquet dived for the inside line, whereupon Patrese shut him off without warning, sending both cars slewing down the track in a welter of wheels, debris and orange flame. Miraculously, neither driver was injured in this spectacular and controversial accident.

Under pressure from Prost, Alboreto slid off course on dropped oil, and the Frenchman was quickly past the Ferrari. A puncture caused by debris at Ste Devote further delayed Alboreto, and he could never quite recover the lost ground.

Having shown his talent in the wet race of 1984, Ayrton Senna was back as part of the Lotus team in 1985 – and took pole position. He led the race for the first 10 laps until the car's Renault turbo engine failed. Right, classic view of Monaco from the top of the hill; Stefan Johansson had plenty of time to look at it, for his Ferrari retired after a start-line collision.

Principality personalities – Niki Lauda, below, in the cockpit of the all-conquering McLaren MP4; left, from the top, Alain Prost, Jacques Laffite and Keke Rosberg. Right, Alfa leads Renault round the Loews hairpin. Car 23 is Eddie Cheever's Alfa Romeo, an early retirement from the 1985 race.

1986

McLaren Streets Ahead

From the start of practice to the end of the race, Alain Prost left no-one in any doubt as to his commitment or his superiority. Barring sheer misfortune, the best driver in the best car will always outrun the opposition; and this weekend, Prost and the immaculate McLaren team, fast and sure, left nothing to the whims of fortune.

Competing for the 20 places on the grid, the 26 entries found the circuit changed since 1985 in two respects. The ever-troublesome chicane was now a clearly-defined left-right S-bend, while the exit from La Rascasse had also been remodelled.

Predictably, Prost led the race from start to finish, totally unchallenged. It was an impressive display, but the McLaren-TAG supremacy left little scope for an interesting Grand Prix. From a disappointing ninth position on the grid, Rosberg, in the second McLaren, used grim determination and McLaren reliability to commandeer second place at a circuit not ideally suited to his aggressive driving style.

With the lead beyond dispute, mid-race interest centred on the battle for sixth place between Piquet, Brundle and Tambay. On lap 68, the excitement curdled into horror as Tambay's Lola somersaulted over the top of Brundle's Tyrrell at the Mirabeau and nearly vaulted the guardrails. Thankfully, neither Brundle nor Tambay was hurt, but mere inches had separated Tambay and the spectators from disaster. Prost cruised on to a perfect victory, wildly acclaimed by the crowd.

Left, Michele Alboreto in the Ferrari round Loews. The year before he had posed a strong challenge to Prost, but this time he retired at mid-distance. Nigel Mansell, right, who invariably enjoys Monaco, finished fourth in the Williams-Honda.

Though Prost's McLaren led throughout, except for a pit stop for fresh tyres, new team-mate Keke Rosberg, below, recovered from a poor grid position to present the strongest challenge to him during the race. Ayrton Senna, right, was third in practice and in the race with his Renault-powered Lotus.

163

Rene Arnoux's Ligier passed Thierry Boutsen's Arrows early in the 1986 race and went on to finish fifth, three places and two laps ahead. Advertising on bodywork is an increasingly prominent feature of the Grand Prix scene, and rarely more effectively than in the pits at Monaco, left.

As more drivers made Monaco their home, another dimension in speed was added to their leisure – powerboats. During the 1986 race weekend Elio De Angelis delighted in taking friends and colleagues for a blast in his Cigarette *Typhoon*. Tragically, a few days later De Angelis was dead, killed in testing for Brabham at the Circuit Paul Ricard.

1987

Senna Takes an Active Interest

The unwieldy 24-car grid was more technically diverse this year than any we had seen at recent Monaco Grands Prix. Under the revised F1 rules, normally-aspirated engines of 3.5 litres capacity could now compete against 1.5-litre turbo units emasculated by a 4-bar boost restriction, with the result that a third of the field now eschewed turbo power. Two teams – Lotus and Williams – entered cars with active suspension.

For all that Monaco is a low-speed acceleration and handling circuit, best practice times fell once again to the turbo cars. Foremost non-turbo qualifier was Thierry Boutsen's Benetton-Ford in ninth position, over 3.5 seconds slower than Mansell's pole-winning lap in the Williams-Honda.

From a superb start, Mansell pulled out 10 seconds on Senna and the rest of the field by lap 15. Piquet's Williams lay third, ahead of the Ferrari of Alboreto, who was lucky to be driving at all after a terrifying practice crash. Mansell's Monaco luck persisted, and he duly retired on lap 29 with a holed exhaust, handing the lead to Senna. The Brazilian, fast and flawless in the actively-suspended Lotus, never looked like losing, and Piquet, no street fighter, followed him round disconsolately in second place.

With few accidents, half the field were still running at the end, and the 3.5-litre cars of Jonathan Palmer and Ivan Capelli finished fifth and sixth. Sanity had prevailed.

Left, Alex Caffi was one of 1987's hard triers with the Alfa Romeo turbo-powered Osella. Ayrton Senna's first Monaco Grand Prix win, below, was a first victory for an active-suspension race car. Not much left of Michele Alboreto's Ferrari, right, after a heavy impact during Thursday practice. He was lucky to walk away unscathed.

Souvenir time, left, as Gerhard Berger's Ferrari gets attention in the pits, below. Cheerful but both wheelchair-bound in the Williams pit are Frank Williams and Clay Regazzoni, right. Williams was disabled by a road accident in 1986, Regazzoni after a race accident at Long Beach in 1980.

Stefan Johansson qualified well in the
second McLaren, below, but retired on
the 58th lap. In the unusual shot, right,
Teo Fabi's Benetton-Ford sweeps
round the outside of Philippe Alliot's
Lola-Ford as they drop down through
Mirabeau Inferieur and into Portier en
route for the tunnel.

1988

The Prost and Senna Show

For anyone without a McLaren-Honda — and that meant 24 of the drivers on the grid — the prospects looked distinctly bleak. Coming to Monaco with convincing wins in the preceding Grands Prix at Rio and Imola, the Marlboro McLarens of Senna and Prost

were untouchable in practice. Even with the handicap of overheating brakes and a handling imbalance, Prost managed a lap totally beyond the reach of Berger, third fastest and flying, in the Ferrari, while Senna's electrifying pole time of 1min 23.998sec made almost everyone else's efforts seem academic.

Senna wasted no time in stamping his authority on the race. Easily outdragging Prost and Berger to the first corner, he began consolidating his lead by a second a lap. Berger, who had darted past Prost at the start, was probably holding up the McLaren, but overtaking at Monaco is a desperate business, and Alain could do little except peer through the Ferrari's aerofoil as his team-mate diminished to a speck in the distance. Behind these two, Alboreto in the Ferrari fought to keep Mansell's Williams at bay – until lap 33, when Alboreto punted the Williams into retirement. At last, on lap 54, Prost scraped past Berger and set off after Senna, but there seemed no realistic chance of the leader being caught, with over 46 seconds in hand.

Then, suddenly, with 11 laps to go, Prost raced past on his own. Senna did not appear and, in fact, so far as this race was concerned, no-one ever saw him again. The McLaren was in the Armco at Portier, the driver indignant but unhurt. While Senna left the circuit, Prost cruised serenely on to his fourth Monaco victory, only the two Ferraris being fleet enough to see the flag from the same lap.

There is invariably a traffic jam around Loews hairpin on the first lap of the Grand Prix. This is how the field formed single file in 1988.

Left, Berger (Ferrari) leads Prost (McLaren-Honda) during their long duel, but the positions were reversed at the end. Below, Piquet (Lotus-Honda) through the chicane during practice; he went no further than the first corner in the race.

Alessandro Nannini (Benetton-Ford), left, qualified sixth but spun out of the race. Below, Yannick Dalmas was overtaken for sixth place on the last lap; he had trouble getting by his Larrousse-Calmels Lola team-mate Philippe Alliot.

Ayrton Senna, with the race in his pocket and only 12 laps to go, made a rare unforced error after McLaren team manager Ron Dennis had radioed to him to slow down. Team-mate Prost went through to win.

Prost chasing Berger down to the waterfront, below, and right, Thierry Boutsen (Benetton-Ford) through Rascasse. The Belgian could not match the speed of team-mate Nannini at this race, but unlike him survived to the finish, in eighth place.

Winners and Losers

The following are the official finishers of all 46 Monaco Grands Prix held between 1929 and 1988. From 1933 onwards, the last two entries for each finisher show grid position and fastest practice time, respectively. Prior to 1933, starting positions were drawn by lot and there was no system of qualification.

1929
1 'Williams' (Bugatti) 49.83mph
2 E. Bouriano (Bugatti)
3 R. Caracciola (Mercedes-Benz)
4 P. de Rothschild (Bugatti)
5 R. Dreyfus (Bugatti)
6 P. Etancelin (Bugatti)
7 M. Lepori (Bugatti)
8 M. Doré (la Licorne)
9 L. Rigal (Alfa Romeo)
Fastest lap: 'Williams' – 2min 15sec, 52.69mph
Winning margin: 1min 17.8sec

1930
1 R. Dreyfus (Bugatti) 53.64mph
2 L. Chiron (Bugatti)
3 G. Bouriat (Bugatti)
4 G. Zehender (Bugatti)
5 M. Doré (Bugatti)
6 H. Stuber (Bugatti)
Fastest lap: Dreyfus – 2min 7sec, 56.01mph
Winning margin: 21.8sec

1931
1 L. Chiron (Bugatti) 54.09mph
2 L. Fagioli (Maserati)
3 A. Varzi (Bugatti)
4 G. Bouriat (Bugatti)
5 G. Zehender (Alfa Romeo)
6 A. Boillot (Peugeot)
7 C. Biondetti (Maserati)
8 C. Penn-Hughes (Bugatti)
9 S. Czaikowski (Bugatti)
Fastest lap: Chiron, Fagioli and Varzi –
2min 7sec, 56.01mph
Winning margin: 1min 55.4sec

1932
1 T. Nuvolari (Alfa Romeo) 55.81mph
2 R. Caracciola (Alfa Romeo)
3 L. Fagioli (Maserati)
4 E. Howe (Bugatti)
5 G. Zehender (Alfa Romeo)
6 M. Lehoux (Bugatti)
7 'Williams' (Bugatti)
8 G. Bouriat (Bugatti)
9 A. Divo (Bugatti)
10 G. Campari (Alfa Romeo)
Fastest lap: Varzi (Bugatti) – 2min 2sec, 58.31mph
Winning margin: 2.7sec

1933
1 A. Varzi (Bugatti) 56.45mph   1   2min 2sec
2 B. Borzacchini (Alfa Romeo)   3   2min 3sec
3 R. Dreyfus (Bugatti)   6   2min 5sec
4 L. Chiron (Alfa Romeo)   2   2min 8sec
5 C. Trossi (Alfa Romeo)   10   2min 8sec
6 G. Zehender (Maserati)   11   2min 8sec
7 'Williams' (Bugatti)   14   2min 11sec
8 L. Hartmann (Bugatti)   18   2min 22sec
Fastest lap: Varzi – 1min 59.0sec, 59.77mph
Winning margin: 12.0sec

1934
1 G. Moll (Alfa Romeo) 56.05mph   7   2min 00sec
2 L. Chiron (Alfa Romeo)   6   2min 00sec
3 R. Dreyfus (Bugatti)   3   1min 59sec
4 M. Lehoux (Alfa Romeo)   10   2min 00sec
5 T. Nuvolari (Bugatti)   5   1min 59sec
6 A. Varzi (Alfa Romeo)   4   1min 59sec
7 W. Straight (Maserati)   11   2min 2sec
8 E. Siena (Maserati)   12   2min 5sec
9 P. Veyron (Bugatti)   14   2min 6sec
10 E. Howe (Maserati)   15   2min 8sec
Fastest lap: Trossi (Alfa Romeo) – 2min 00sec, 59.28mph
Fastest in practice: Trossi – 1min 58sec
Winning margin: 1min 2.0sec

1935
1 L. Fagioli (Mercedes-Benz)
58.17mph   3   1min 57.3sec
2 R. Dreyfus (Alfa Romeo)   4   1min 59.0sec
3 A Brivio (Alfa Romeo)   6   2min 1.0sec
4 P. Etancelin (Maserati)   9   2min 2.2sec
5 L. Chiron (Alfa Romeo)   7   2min 1.8sec
6 R. Sommer (Alfa Romeo)   8   2min 2.0sec
7 G. Zehender (Maserati)   10   2min 4.0sec
8 G. Soffietti (Maserati)   13   2min 5.1sec
Fastest lap: Fagioli – 1min 58.4sec, 60.18mph
Fastest in practice: Caracciola (Mercedes-Benz) –
1min 56.6sec
Winning margin: 32.5sec

1936
1 R. Caracciola (Mercedes-Benz)
51.69mph   3   1min 54.0sec
2 A. Varzi (Auto Union)   7   1min 56.1sec
3 H. Stuck (Auto Union)   4   1min 54.3sec
4 T. Nuvolari (Alfa Romeo)   2   1min 53.7sec
5 A. Brivio*/G. Farina
(Alfa Romeo)   11   1min 58.0sec*
6 J-P. Wimille (Bugatti)   8   1min 56.6sec
7 R. Sommer (Alfa Romeo)   14   2min 3.3sec
8 P. Ghersi (Maserati)   17   2min 8.7sec
9 'Williams' (Bugatti)   16   2min 5.0sec
Fastest lap: Stuck – 2min 7.4sec, 55.86mph
Fastest in practice: Chiron (Mercedes-Benz) –
1min 53.2sec
Winning margin: 1min 48.9sec

1937

1	M. von Brauchitsch			
	(Mercedes-Benz) 63.27mph	2	1min 48.4sec	
2	R. Caracciola (Mercedes-Benz)	1	1min 47.5sec	
3	C. Kautz (Mercedes-Benz)	5	1min 49.7sec	
4	H. Stuck*/B. Rosemeyer			
	(Auto Union)	4	1min 49.2sec*	
5	G. Zehender (Mercedes-Benz)	7	1min 53.3sec	
6	G. Farina (Alfa Romeo)	8	1min 53.4sec	
7	R. Sommer (Alfa Romeo)	12	1min 57.6sec	
8	H. Ruesch (Alfa Romeo)	10	1min 55.8sec	
9	C. Pintacuda (Alfa Romeo)	9	1min 55.6sec	

Fastest lap: Caracciola – 1min 46.5sec, 66.79mph
Winning margin: 1min 25.3sec

1948

1	G. Farina (Maserati) 59.74mph	1	1min 53.8sec	
2	L. Chiron (Talbot)	11	2min 0.4sec	
3	T. de Graffenried (Maserati)	7	1min 58.1sec	
4	M. Trintignant (Simca-Gordini)	13	–	
5	L. Villoresi*/A. Ascari (Maserati)	3	1min 54.3sec*	
6	Y. Giraud-Cabantous (Talbot)	12	–	
7	E. Chaboud (Delahaye)	19	–	
8	C. Bucci (Maserati)	8	1min 59.7sec	

Fastest lap: Farina – 1min 53.9sec, 62.67mph
Winning margin: 36.2sec

1950

1	J-M. Fangio (Alfa Romeo)			
	61.33mph	1	1min 50.2sec	
2	A. Ascari (Ferrari)	7	1min 53.8sec	
3	L. Chiron (Maserati)	8	1min 56.3sec	
4	R. Sommer (Ferrari)	9	1min 56.6sec	
5	B. Bira (Maserati)	15	2min 2.2sec	
6	F. Gerard (ERA)	16	2min 3.4sec	
7	J. Claes (Talbot)	18	2min 12.0sec	

Fastest lap: Fangio – 1min 51.0sec, 64.09mph
Winning margin: 1 lap

1952

1	V. Marzotto (Ferrari) 58.20mph	11	2min 3.2sec	
2	E. Castellotti (Ferrari)	10	2min 2.9sec	
3	A. Stagnoli (Ferrari)	3	2min 0.7sec	
4	J. Lucas (Ferrari)	15	2min 6.9sec	
5	P. Pagnibon (Ferrari)	8	2min 2.2sec	
6	T. Wisdom (Jaguar)	16	2min 9.0sec	
7	P. Collins (Aston Martin)	12	2min 3.5sec	
8	R. Cotton (Delahaye)	18	2min 10.2sec	

Fastest lap: Stagnoli – 1min 56.4sec, 60.4mph
Fastest in practice: Levegh (Talbot) – 2min 0.2sec
Winning margin: 15.2sec

1955

1	M. Trintignant (Ferrari)			
	65.63mph	9	1min 44.4sec	
2	E. Castellotti (Lancia)	4	1min 42.0sec	
3	J. Behra (Maserati)	5	1min 42.6sec	
4	G. Farina (Ferrari)	14	1min 46.0sec	
5	L. Villoresi (Lancia)	7	1min 43.7sec	
6	L. Chiron (Lancia)	19	1min 47.3sec	
7	J. Pollet (Gordini)	20	1min 49.4sec	
8	P. Taruffi*/P. Frère (Ferrari)	15	1min 46.0sec*	
9	S. Moss (Mercedes-Benz)	3	1min 41.2sec	

Fastest lap: Fangio (Mercedes-Benz) –
1min 42.4sec, 68.69mph
Fastest in practice: Fangio – 1min 41.1sec
Winning margin: 20.3sec

1956

1	S. Moss (Maserati) 64.95mph	2	1min 44.6sec	
2	P. Collins (Ferrari)	9	1min 47.0sec	
3	J. Behra (Maserati)	4	1min 45.3sec	
4	J-M. Fangio (Ferrari)	1	1min 44.0sec	
5	H-J. da Silva Ramos (Gordini)	10	1min 50.0sec	
6	E. Bayol (Gordini)	12	1min 50.6sec	
7	C. Perdisa (Maserati)	7	1min 46.0sec	
8	H. Gould (Maserati)	14	1min 51.7sec	

Fastest lap: Fangio – 1min 44.4sec, 67.39mph
Winning margin: 6.1sec

1957

1	J-M. Fangio (Maserati) 64.75mph	1	1min 42.7sec	
2	T. Brooks (Vanwall)	4	1min 44.4sec	
3	M. Gregory (Maserati)	10	1min 48.4sec	
4	S. Lewis-Evans (Connaught)	13	1min 49.1sec	
5	M. Trintignant (Ferrari)	7	1min 46.7sec	
6	J. Brabham (Cooper-Climax)	15	1min 49.3sec	

Fastest lap: Fangio – 1min 45.6sec, 66.63mph
Winning margin: 25.2sec

1958

1	M. Trintignant (Cooper-Climax)			
		67.98mph	5	1min 41.1sec
2	L. Musso (Ferrari)		10	1min 42.6sec
3	P. Collins (Ferrari)		9	1min 41.5sec
4	J. Brabham (Cooper-Climax)		3	1min 41.0sec
5	H. Schell (BRM)		11	1min 43.8sec
6	C. Allison (Lotus-Climax)		13	1min 44.6sec

Fastest lap: Hawthorn (Ferrari) –
1min 40.6sec, 69.93mph
Fastest in practice: Brooks (Vanwall) – 1min 39.8sec
Winning margin: 20.2 sec

1959

1	J. Brabham (Cooper-Climax)			
		66.74mph	3	1min 40.1sec
2	T. Brooks (Ferrari)		4	1min 41.0sec
3	M. Trintignant (Cooper-Climax)		6	1min 41.7sec
4	P. Hill (Ferrari)		5	1min 41.3sec
5	B. McLaren (Cooper-Climax)		13	1min 43.9sec
6	R. Salvadori (Cooper-Maserati)		8	1min 42.4sec

Fastest lap: Brabham – 1min 40.4sec, 70.07mph
Fastest in practice: Moss (Cooper-Climax) –
1min 39.6sec
Winning margin: 20.4sec

1960

1	S. Moss (Lotus-Climax)			
		67.46mph	1	1min 36.3sec
2	B. McLaren (Cooper-Climax)		11	1min 38.6sec
3	P. Hill (Ferrari)		10	1min 38.6sec
4	T. Brooks (Cooper-Climax)		3	1min 37.7sec
5	J. Bonnier (BRM)		5	1min 37.7sec
6	R. Ginther (Ferrari)		9	1min 38.6sec
7	G. Hill (BRM)		6	1min 38.0sec
8	W. von Trips (Ferrari)		8	1min 38.3sec
9	I. Ireland (Lotus-Climax)		7	1min 38.2sec

Fastest lap: McLaren – 1min 36.2sec, 73.13mph
Winning margin: 52.1sec

1961

1	S. Moss (Lotus-Climax)			
		70.70mph	1	1min 39.1sec
2	R. Ginther (Ferrari)		2	1min 39.3sec
3	P. Hill (Ferrari)		5	1min 39.8sec
4	W. von Trips (Ferrari)		6	1min 39.8sec
5	D. Gurney (Porsche)		10	1min 40.6sec
6	B. McLaren (Cooper-Climax)		7	1min 39.8sec

7	M. Trintignant (Cooper-Maserati)	*15*	1min 42.4sec
8	C. Allison (Lotus-Climax)	*14*	1min 42.3sec
9	H. Herrmann (Porsche)	*12*	1min 41.1sec
10	J. Clark (Lotus-Climax)	*3*	1min 39.6sec
11	J. Surtees (Cooper-Climax)	*11*	1min 41.1sec
12	J. Bonnier (Porsche)	*9*	1min 40.3sec
13	T. Brooks (BRM-Climax)	*8*	1min 40.1sec

Fastest lap: Ginther and Moss – 1min 36.3sec, 73.05mph
Winning margin: 3.6sec

1962

1	B. McLaren (Cooper-Climax)			
		70.46mph	3	1min 36.4sec
2	P. Hill (Ferrari)		9	1min 37.1sec
3	L. Bandini (Ferrari)		10	1min 37.2sec
4	J. Surtees (Lola-Climax)		11	1min 37.9sec
5	J. Bonnier (Porsche)		15	1min 42.4sec
6	G. Hill (BRM)		2	1min 35.8sec
7	W. Mairesse (Ferrari)		4	1min 36.4sec
8	J. Brabham (Lotus-Climax)		6	1min 36.5sec

Fastest lap: Clark (Lotus-Climax) –
1min 35.5sec, 73.67mph
Fastest in practice: Clark – 1min 35.4sec
Winning margin: 1.3sec

1963

1	G. Hill (BRM) 72.42mph		2	1min 35.0sec
2	R. Ginther (BRM)		4	1min 35.2sec
3	B. McLaren (Cooper-Climax)		8	1min 36.0sec
4	J. Surtees (Ferrari)		3	1min 35.2sec
5	T. Maggs (Cooper-Climax)		10	1min 37.9sec
6	T. Taylor (Lotus-Climax)		9	1min 37.2sec
7	J. Bonnier (Cooper-Climax)		11	1min 38.6sec
8	J. Clark (Lotus-Climax)		1	1min 34.3sec
9	J. Brabham (Lotus-Climax)		15	1min 44.7sec

Fastest lap: Surtees – 1min 34.5sec, 74.45mph
Winning margin: 4.6 sec

1964

1	G. Hill (BRM) 72.64mph		3	1min 34.5sec
2	R. Ginther (BRM)		8	1min 35.9sec
3	P. Arundell (Lotus-Climax)		6	1min 35.5sec
4	J. Clark (Lotus-Climax)		1	1min 34.0sec
5	J. Bonnier (Cooper-Climax)		11	1min 37.4sec
6	M. Hailwood (Lotus-BRM)		15	1min 38.5sec
7	R. Anderson (Brabham-Climax)		12	1min 38.0sec
8	J. Siffert (Lotus-BRM)		16	1min 38.7sec
9	P. Hill (Cooper-Climax)		9	1min 35.9sec

Fastest lap: G. Hill – 1min 33.9sec, 74.92mph
Winning margin: 1 lap

1965
1	G. Hill (BRM) 74.34mph	1	1min 32.5sec
2	L. Bandini (Ferrari)	4	1min 33.0sec
3	J. Stewart (BRM)	3	1min 32.9sec
4	J. Surtees (Ferrari)	5	1min 33.2sec
5	B. McLaren (Cooper-Climax)	7	1min 34.3sec
6	J. Siffert (Brabham-BRM)	10	1min 36.0sec
7	J. Bonnier (Brabham-Climax)	13	1min 36.7sec
8	D. Hulme (Brabham-Climax)	8	1min 34.8sec
9	R. Anderson (Brabham-Climax)	9	1min 35.5sec

Fastest lap: Hill – 1min 31.7sec, 76.72mph
Winning margin: 1min 4.0sec

1966
1	J. Stewart (BRM) 77.29mph	3	1min 30.3sec
2	L. Bandini (Ferrari)	5	1min 30.5sec
3	G. Hill (BRM)	4	1min 30.4sec
4	B. Bondurant (BRM)	16	1min 37.3sec

Fastest lap: Bandini – 1min 29.8sec, 78.34mph
Fastest in practice: Clark (Lotus-Climax)–1min 29.9sec
Winning margin: 40.2sec

1967
1	D. Hulme (Brabham-Repco) 76.68mph	4	1min 28.8sec
2	G. Hill (Lotus-BRM)	8	1min 29.9sec
3	C. Amon (Ferrari)	14	1min 30.7sec
4	B. McLaren (McLaren-BRM)	10	1min 30.0sec
5	P. Rodriguez (Cooper-Maserati)	16	1min 32.4sec
6	M. Spence (BRM)	12	1min 30.6sec

Fastest lap: Clark (Lotus-Climax) – 1min 29.5sec, 78.60mph
Fastest in practice: Brabham (Brabham-Repco) – 1min 27.6sec
Winning margin: 1 lap

1968
1	G. Hill (Lotus-Ford) 77.82mph	1	1min 28.2sec
2	R. Attwood (BRM)	6	1min 29.6sec
3	L. Bianchi (Cooper-BRM)	14	1min 31.9sec
4	L. Scarfiotti (Cooper-BRM)	15	1min 32.9sec
5	D. Hulme (McLaren-Ford)	10	1min 30.4sec

Fastest lap: Attwood – 1min 28.1sec, 79.92mph
Winning margin: 2.2sec

1969
1	G. Hill (Lotus-Ford) 80.18mph	4	1min 25.8sec
2	P. Courage (Brabham-Ford)	9	1min 26.4sec
3	J. Siffert (Lotus-Ford)	5	1min 26.0sec
4	R. Attwood (Lotus-Ford)	10	1min 26.5sec
5	B. McLaren (McLaren-Ford)	11	1min 26.7sec
6	D. Hulme (McLaren-Ford)	12	1min 26.8sec
7	V. Elford (Cooper-Maserati)	16	1min 32.8sec

Fastest lap: Courage – 1min 25.8sec, 81.99mph
Fastest in practice: Stewart (Matra-Ford) – 1min 24.6sec
Winning margin: 17.3sec

1970
1	J. Rindt (Lotus-Ford) 81.84mph	8	1min 25.9sec
2	J. Brabham (Brabham-Ford)	4	1min 25.4sec
3	H. Pescarolo (Matra-Simca)	7	1min 25.7sec
4	D. Hulme (McLaren-Ford)	3	1min 25.1sec
5	G. Hill (Lotus-Ford)	16	–
6	P. Rodriguez (BRM)	15	1min 28.8sec
7	R. Peterson (March-Ford)	12	1min 26.8sec
8	J. Siffert (March-Ford)	11	1min 26.2sec
9	P. Courage (De Tomaso-Ford)	9	1min 26.1sec

Fastest lap: Rindt – 1min 23.2sec, 84.56mph
Fastest in practice: Stewart (March-Ford) – 1min 24.0sec
Winning margin: 23.2sec

1971
1	J. Stewart (Tyrrell-Ford) 83.49mph		1min 23.2sec
2	R. Peterson (March-Ford)	8	1min 25.8sec
3	J. Ickx (Ferrari)	2	1min 24.2sec
4	D. Hulme (McLaren-Ford)	6	1min 25.3sec
5	E. Fittipaldi (Lotus-Ford)	17	1min 27.7sec
6	R. Stommelen (Surtees-Ford)	16	1min 27.2sec
7	J. Surtees (Surtees-Ford)	10	1min 26.0sec
8	H. Pescarolo (March-Ford)	13	1min 26.7sec
9	P. Rodriguez (BRM)	5	1min 25.1sec
10	T. Schenken (Brabham-Ford)	18	1min 28.3sec

Fastest lap: Stewart – 1min 22.2sec, 85.58mph
Winning margin: 25.6sec

1972
1	J-P. Beltoise (BRM) 63.85mph	4	1min 22.5sec
2	J. Ickx (Ferrari)	2	1min 21.6sec
3	E. Fittipaldi (Lotus-Ford)	1	1min 21.4sec
4	J. Stewart (Tyrrell-Ford)	8	1min 22.9sec
5	B. Redman (McLaren-Ford)	10	1min 23.1sec
6	C. Amon (Matra-Simca)	6	1min 22.6sec
7	A. de Adamich (Surtees-Ford)	18	1min 24.7sec

8	H. Marko (BRM)	17	1min 24.6sec
9	W. Fittipaldi (Brabham-Ford)	21	1min 25.2sec
10	R. Stommelen (March-Ford)	25	1min 29.5sec
11	R. Peterson (March-Ford)	15	1min 24.1sec
12	G. Hill (Brabham-Ford)	19	1min 24.7sec
13	M. Beuttler (March-Ford)	23	1min 26.5sec
14	D. Walker (Lotus-Ford)	14	1min 24.0sec
15	D. Hulme (McLaren-Ford)	7	1min 22.7sec
16	N. Lauda (March-Ford)	22	1min 25.6sec
17	C. Pace (March-Ford)	24	1min 26.6sec

Fastest lap: Beltoise – 1min 40.0sec, 70.35mph

Winning margin: 38.2 sec

1973

1	J. Stewart (Tyrrell-Ford)		
	80.96mph	1	1min 27.5sec
2	E. Fittipaldi (Lotus-Ford)	5	1min 28.1sec
3	R. Peterson (Lotus-Ford)	2	1min 27.7sec
4	F. Cevert (Tyrrell-Ford)	4	1min 27.9sec
5	P. Revson (McLaren-Ford)	15	1min 29.4sec
6	D. Hulme (McLaren-Ford)	3	1min 27.8sec
7	A. de Adamich (Brabham-Ford)	25	1min 32.1sec
8	M. Hailwood (Surtees-Ford)	13	1min 29.4sec
9	J. Hunt (March-Ford)	18	1min 29.9sec
10	J. Oliver (Shadow-Ford)	22	1min 31.2sec
11	W. Fittipaldi (Brabham-Ford)	9	1min 28.9sec

Fastest lap: E. Fittipaldi – 1min 28.1sec, 83.23mph

Winning margin: 1.3sec

1974

1	R. Peterson (Lotus-Ford)		
	80.74mph	3	1min 26.8sec
2	J. Scheckter (Tyrrell-Ford)	4	1min 27.1sec
3	J-P. Jarier (Shadow-Ford)	5	1min 27.5sec
4	C. Regazzoni (Ferrari)	2	1min 26.6sec
5	E. Fittipaldi (McLaren-Ford)	12	1min 28.2sec
6	J. Watson (Brabham-Ford)	21	1min 30.0sec
7	G. Hill (Lola-Ford)	19	1min 30.0sec
8	G. Edwards (Lola-Ford)	22	1min 30.4sec
9	P. Depailler (Tyrrell-Ford)	24	1min 27.1sec

Fastest lap: Peterson – 1min 27.9sec, 83.42mph

Fastest in practice: Lauda (Ferrari) – 1 min 26.3sec

Winning margin: 28.8sec

1975

1	N. Lauda (Ferrari) 75.53mph	1	1min 26.40sec
2	E. Fittipaldi (McLaren-Ford)	9	1min 27.77sec
3	C. Pace (Brabham-Ford)	8	1min 27.67sec

4	R. Peterson (Lotus-Ford)	4	1min 27.40sec
5	P. Depailler (Tyrrell-Ford)	12	1min 27.95sec
6	J. Mass (McLaren-Ford)	15	1min 28.49sec
7	J. Scheckter (Tyrrell-Ford)	7	1min 27.58sec
8	J. Ickx (Lotus-Ford)	14	1min 28.28sec
9	C. Reutemann (Brabham-Ford)	10	1min 27.93sec

Fastest lap: Depailler – 1min 28.67sec, 82.70mph

Winning margin: 2.78sec

1976

1	N. Lauda (Ferrari) 80.31mph	1	1min 29.65sec
2	J. Scheckter (Tyrrell-Ford)	5	1min 30.55sec
3	P. Depailler (Tyrrell-Ford)	4	1min 30.33sec
4	H. Stuck (March-Ford)	6	1min 30.60sec
5	J. Mass (McLaren-Ford)	11	1min 31.67sec
6	E. Fittipaldi (Copersucar-Ford)	7	1min 31.39sec
7	T. Pryce (Shadow-Ford)	15	1min 31.98sec
8	J-P. Jarier (Shadow-Ford)	10	1min 31.65sec
9	C. Pace (Brabham-Alfa Romeo)	13	1min 31.81sec
10	J. Watson (Penske-Ford)	17	1min 32.14sec
11	M. Leclere (Williams-Ford)	18	1min 32.17sec
12	J. Laffite (Ligier-Matra)	8	1min 31.46sec
13	C. Amon (Ensign-Ford)	12	1min 31.75sec
14	C. Regazzoni (Ferrari)	2	1min 29.91sec

Fastest lap: Regazzoni – 1min 30.28sec, 82.06mph

Winning margin: 11.13sec

1977

1	J. Scheckter (Wolf-Ford)		
	79.61mph	2	1min 30.27sec
2	N. Lauda (Ferrari)	6	1min 30.76sec
3	C. Reutemann (Ferrari)	3	1min 30.44sec
4	J. Mass (McLaren-Ford)	9	1min 31.36sec
5	M. Andretti (Lotus-Ford)	10	1min 31.50sec
6	A. Jones (Shadow-Ford)	11	1min 32.04sec
7	J. Laffite (Ligier-Matra)	16	1min 32.65sec
8	V. Brambilla (Surtees-Ford)	14	1min 32.40sec
9	R. Patrese (Shadow-Ford)	15	1min 32.52sec
10	J. Ickx (Ensign-Ford)	17	1min 33.25sec
11	J-P. Jarier (Hesketh-Ford)	12	1min 32.32sec
12	R. Keegan (Hesketh-Ford)	20	1min 33.78sec

Fastest lap: Scheckter – 1min 31.07sec, 81.35mph

Fastest in practice: Watson (Brabham-Alfa Romeo) – 1min 29.86sec

Winning margin: 0.89sec

1978

1	P. Depailler (Tyrrell-Ford)		
	80.36mph	5	1min 29.14sec

2	N. Lauda (Brabham-Alfa Romeo)	3	1min 28.84sec
3	J. Scheckter (Wolf-Ford)	9	1min 29.50sec
4	J. Watson (Brabham-AlfaRomeo)	2	1min 28.83sec
5	D. Pironi (Tyrrell-Ford)	13	1min 30.55sec
6	R. Patrese (Arrows-Ford)	14	1min 30.59sec
7	P. Tambay (McLaren-Ford)	11	1min 30.08sec
8	C. Reutemann (Ferrari)	1	1min 28.34sec
9	E. Fittipaldi (Copersucar-Ford)	20	1min 31.36sec
10	J-P. Jabouille (Renault)	12	1min 30.18sec
11	M. Andretti (Lotus-Ford)	4	1min 29.10sec

Fastest lap: Lauda – 1min 28.65sec, 83.57mph

Winning margin: 22.35sec

1979

1	J. Scheckter (Ferrari) 81.34mph	1	1min 26.45sec
2	C. Regazzoni (Williams-Ford)	16	1min 28.48sec
3	C. Reutemann (Lotus-Ford)	11	1min 27.99sec
4	J. Watson (McLaren-Ford)	14	1min 28.23sec
5	P. Depailler (Ligier-Ford)	3	1min 27.11sec
6	J. Mass (Arrows-Ford)	8	1min 27.47sec
7	N. Piquet (Brabham-AlfaRomeo)	18	1min 28.52sec
8	J-P. Jabouille (Renault)	20	1min 28.68sec

Fastest lap: Depailler – 1min 28.82sec, 82.17mph

Winning margin: 0.44sec

1980

1	C. Reutemann (Williams-Ford) 81.20mph	2	1min 24.88sec
2	J. Laffite (Ligier-Ford)	5	1min 25.51sec
3	N. Piquet (Brabham-Ford)	4	1min 25.36sec
4	J. Mass (Arrows-Ford)	15	1min 26.96sec
5	G. Villeneuve (Ferrari)	6	1min 26.10sec
6	E. Fittipaldi (Fittipaldi-Ford)	18	1min 27.49sec
7	M. Andretti (Lotus-Ford)	19	1min 27.51sec
8	R. Patrese (Arrows-Ford)	11	1min 26.83sec

Fastest lap: Reutemann – 1min 27.418sec, 84.75mph
Fastest in practice: Pironi (Ferrari) – 1min 24.81sec
Winning margin: 1min 13.63sec

1981

1	G. Villeneuve (Ferrari) 82.04mph	2	1min 25.78sec
2	A. Jones (Williams-Ford)	7	1min 26.53sec
3	J. Laffite (Ligier-Matra)	8	1min 26.70sec
4	D. Pironi (Ferrari)	17	1min 28.26sec
5	E. Cheever (Tyrrell-Ford)	15	1min 27.59sec
6	M. Surer (Ensign-Ford)	19	1min 28.33sec
7	P. Tambay (Theodore-Ford)	16	1min 27.93sec

Fastest lap: Jones – 1min 27.47sec, 84.70mph
Fastest in practice: Piquet (Brabham-Ford) – 1min 25.71sec

Winning margin: 39.90sec

1982

1	R. Patrese (Brabham-Ford) 82.21mph	2	1min 23.79sec
2	D. Pironi (Ferrari)	5	1min 24.59sec
3	A. de Cesaris (Alfa Romeo)	7	1min 24.93sec
4	N. Mansell (Lotus-Ford)	11	1min 25.64sec
5	E. De Angelis (Lotus-Ford)	15	1min 26.46sec
6	D. Daly (Williams-Ford)	8	1min 25.39sec
7	A. Prost (Renault)	4	1min 24.44sec
8	B. Henton (Tyrrell-Ford)	17	1min 26.69sec
9	M. Surer (Arrows-Ford)	19	1min 27.02sec
10	M. Alboreto (Tyrrell-Ford)	9	1min 25.45sec

Fastest lap: Patrese – 1min 26.35sec, 85.79mph
Fastest in practice: Arnoux (Renault) – 1min 23.28sec
Winning margin: 1 lap

1983

1	K. Rosberg (Williams-Ford) 80.52mph	5	1min 26.31sec
2	N. Piquet (Brabham-BMW)	6	1min 27.27sec
3	A. Prost (Renault)	1	1min 24.84sec

4	P. Tambay (Ferrari)	4	1min 26.30sec
5	D. Sullivan (Tyrrell-Ford)	20	1min 29.53sec
6	M. Baldi (Alfa Romeo)	13	1min 28.64sec
7	C. Serra (Arrows-Ford)	15	1min 28.78sec

Fastest lap: Piquet – 1min 27.28sec, 84.88mph
Winning margin: 18.48sec

1984

1	A. Prost (McLaren-TAG Porsche) 62.62mph	1	1min 22.66sec
2	A. Senna (Toleman-Hart)	13	1min 25.01sec
3	S. Bellof (Tyrrell-Ford)	20	1min 26.12sec
4	R. Arnoux (Ferrari)	3	1min 22.93sec
5	K. Rosberg (Williams-Honda)	10	1min 24.15sec
6	E. De Angelis (Lotus-Renault)	11	1min 24.43sec
7	M. Alboreto (Ferrari)	4	1min 22.94sec
8	P. Ghinzani (Osella-Alfa Romeo)	19	1min 25.88sec
9	J. Laffite (Williams-Honda)	16	1min 25.72sec

Fastest lap: Senna – 1min 54.33sec, 64.80mph
Winning margin: 7.45sec

1985

1	A. Prost (McLaren-TAG Porsche) 86.02mph	5	1min 20.88sec
2	M. Alboreto (Ferrari)	3	1min 20.54sec
3	E. De Angelis (Lotus-Renault)	9	1min 21.46sec
4	A. de Cesaris (Ligier-Renault)	8	1min 21.35sec
5	D. Warwick (Renault)	10	1min 21.53sec
6	J. Laffite (Ligier-Renault)	16	1min 22.88sec
7	N. Mansell (Williams-Honda)	2	1min 20.54sec
8	K. Rosberg (Williams-Honda)	7	1min 21.32sec
9	T. Boutsen (Arrows-BMW)	6	1min 21.30sec
10	M. Brundle (Tyrrell-Ford)	18	1min 23.83sec
11	J. Palmer (Zakspeed)	19	1min 23.84sec

Fastest lap: Alboreto – 1min 22.64sec, 89.66mph
Fastest in practice: Senna (Lotus-Renault) – 1min 20.45sec
Winning margin: 7.54sec

1986

1	A. Prost (McLaren-TAG Porsche) 83.65mph	1	1min 22.63sec
2	K. Rosberg (McLaren-TAG Porsche)	9	1min 24.70sec
3	A. Senna (Lotus-Renault)	3	1min 23.17sec
4	N. Mansell (Williams-Honda)	2	1min 23.05sec
5	R. Arnoux (Ligier-Renault)	12	1min 25.54sec
6	J. Laffite (Ligier-Renault)	7	1min 24.40sec
7	N. Piquet (Williams-Honda)	11	1min 25.29sec
8	T. Boutsen (Arrows-BMW)	14	1min 25.83sec
9	M. Surer (Arrows-BMW)	17	1min 26.30sec
10	S. Johansson (Ferrari)	15	1min 25.91sec
11	P. Streiff (Tyrrell-Renault)	13	1min 25.72sec
12	J. Palmer (Zakspeed)	19	1min 26.64sec

Fastest lap: Prost – 1min 26.61sec, 85.95mph
Winning margin: 25.02sec

1987

1	A. Senna (Lotus-Honda) 81.69mph	2	1min 23.71sec
2	N. Piquet (Williams-Honda)	3	1min 24.76sec
3	M. Alboreto (Ferrari)	5	1min 26.10sec
4	G. Berger (Ferrari)	8	1min 26.32sec
5	J. Palmer (Tyrrell-Ford)	15	1min 28.09sec
6	I. Capelli (March-Ford)	19	1min 29.15sec
7	M. Brundle (Zakspeed)	14	1min 27.89sec
8	T. Fabi (Benetton-Ford)	12	1min 27.62sec
9	A. Prost (McLaren-TAG Porsche)	4	1min 25.08sec
10	S. Nakajima (Lotus-Honda)	17	1min 28.89sec
11	R. Arnoux (Ligier-Megatron)	22	1min 30.00sec
12	P. Ghinzani (Ligier-Megatron)	20	1min 29.26sec
13	P. Fabre (AGS-Ford)	25	1min 31.67sec

Fastest lap: Senna – 1min 27.68sec, 84.90mph
Fastest in practice: Mansell (Williams-Honda) – 1min 23.04sec
Winning margin: 33.21sec

1988

1	A. Prost (McLaren-Honda) 82.52mph	2	1min 25.42sec
2	G. Berger (Ferrari)	3	1min 26.68sec
3	M. Alboreto (Ferrari)	4	1min 27.30sec
4	D. Warwick (Arrows-Megatron)	7	1min 27.87sec
5	J. Palmer (Tyrrell-Ford)	10	1min 28.36sec
6	R. Patrese (Williams-Judd)	8	1min 28.02sec
7	Y. Dalmas (Lola-Ford)	21	1min 29.60sec
8	T. Boutsen (Benetton-Ford)	16	1min 28.64sec
9	N. Larini (Osella-Alfa Romeo)	25	1min 30.33sec
10	I. Capelli (March-Judd)	22	1min 29.60sec

Fastest lap: Senna (McLaren-Honda) – 1min 26.32sec, 86.26mph
Fastest in practice: Senna – 1min 24.00sec
Winning margin: 20.45sec

Photographic Credits

The publishers gratefully acknowledge the following sources for additional photographs used to illustrate this book on the pages noted:

Agence de Presse Rougier, 155

Archives Commission Historique, Automobile Club de France, 31

Archives Département Co-ordination et Preservation du Patrimoine Historique, la Societe des Bains de Mer, Monte Carlo, 21, 29, 30 (lower), 32, 33, 34 (lower), 35 (upper), 36

Archives Palais Princier, Monaco, 20, 30 (upper), 34 (upper), 38 (upper), 41, 42, 43, 46, 47, 49 (upper)

Rene Briano, 74 (top)

Daimler-Benz AG, 39, 40, 44

Geoffrey Goddard, 50 (upper), 51

David Hodges, 9

Keystone (Paris), 35 (lower)

London Art Tech, 38 (lower), 52

Jean-Marie Moll, 14, 15, 24, 70 (upper), 91 (lower), 130 (left)

Motor News & Features, 50 (lower)

Chris Mullen, 18

Quadrant Picture Library, 49 (lower)

Henri Vachon/*Automobile Year* Archive, 45